VOLUME TWO

GIS
means Business

DAVID BOYLES

ESRI PRESS
REDLANDS, CALIFORNIA

ESRI
GIS Means Business, Volume Two
ISBN 1-58948-033-3

First printing May 2002.

Printed in the United States of America.

Library of Congress Catalog Control Number: 99-194842

Published by ESRI, 380 New York Street, Redlands, California 92373-8100.

Books from ESRI Press are available to resellers worldwide through Independent Publishers Group (IPG). For information on volume discounts, or to place an order, call IPG at 1-800-888-4741 in the United States, or at 312-337-0747 outside the United States.

Contents

Other books from ESRI Press

Preface

During the 1990s, geographic information systems (GIS) played a major role in reinventing the business world, and the process continues at a rapid rate.

When *ArcView GIS Means Business* was published by ESRI Press in 1997, the preface to that book noted that GIS had begun to significantly take hold in the private sector in only the previous five years. Since 1997, that movement has accelerated. The development and availability of personal and network computers, GIS software, and data of all kinds has grown exponentially, along with the expertise of the business professionals who use these resources for sales, marketing, site and branch location, advertising, fleet routing, economic development, business education, and other commercial endeavors.

This book, which is intended as either a companion volume to *ArcView GIS Means Business* or as a stand-alone effort, presents a number of stories that describe various applications of GIS technology and how it helps people do business. In some respects, this book is also an extension of *Serving Maps on the Internet,* a 1998 ESRI Press publication; there are several chapters in this new volume highlighting how GIS provides interactive, business-related maps to the millions of people now using the World Wide Web.

The introduction to *GIS Means Business, Volume Two* restates and in some cases duplicates the 1997 book's first chapter in the course of dealing with some fundamental matters, including explanations of why geography is important; the nature of GIS; the map paradigm; the basics of visualizing, analyzing, and presenting data; and other general concepts. Coupled with the real-world business case studies in the earlier ESRI Press books, the additional case studies here in volume two represent an ongoing report of what GIS means—and will continue to mean—to the world of business over the coming years.

Of course, a few volumes of case studies amount to only a flavor of a much bigger story, and the reader is encouraged to see these books as a starting point to developing an even deeper understanding of the topic. References to additional GIS and business resources are readily available in every volume mentioned here, and there are myriad others just clicks away on the Web. Indeed, a recent search for "GIS and business" on a popular Internet search engine produced nearly 370,000 references; a month later the same search produced more than 450,000 offerings. The information is out there, and the potential explorations abound.

Acknowledgments

First and foremost, my thanks to Colleen Schelde, marketing coordinator in ESRI's Industry Solutions department in Redlands, for making initial contacts with many of the sources for the case studies in this book. Colleen's work set the stage for further development of many of the stories that follow, and her efforts are greatly appreciated. Thanks also to some of the Industry Solutions managers and staffers who work alongside Colleen; they include Tony Burns, Lee Burton, and Brad McCallum. Several others at ESRI also provided helpful ideas and support, including Karl Terrey, Marj Dougherty, Matt Artz, Dave Wieseler, Lisa Kensok, Deane Kensok, Merrill Lyew, Nancy Sappington, Jesse Theodore, and Peter Schreiber. At ESRI Business Information Solutions, Brent Roderick provided timely and helpful support. There are several others not listed by name who passed along tips and provided information when it was requested. Sorry to say, not every tip or idea could be turned into a published story here and now, but many thanks to those who offered them.

The stories could not have been told without the patience, generosity, time commitments, and kind cooperation of the companies, schools, organizations, and case-study sources themselves; their names are listed at the conclusion of each chapter. ESRI appreciates their willingness to answer questions, provide explanations, share information, and further the understanding of how GIS plays a key role in business and commerce.

Thanks also to my partners at ESRI Press: Christian Harder and R. W. Greene, for their skillful mentoring and steady guidance; Gary Amdahl and Edie Punt, for their considerate and collaborative editing hands; Jennifer Johnston, for her patient and inspired production and layout work; Tiffany Wilkerson and Michael Hyatt, for their typically eagle-eyed copyediting; and Steve Hegle, whose administrative support was time-saving and invaluable. Thanks also to Steve Frizzell of ESRI's Graphics team, who designed the cover, and Cliff Crabbe, who oversaw print production.

Finally, I'm grateful to Judy Boyd and Nick Frunzi in Educational Services for giving me the opportunity to work at ESRI, and to Jack Dangermond, for his vision, invention, and inspiration.

David Boyles
ESRI Press

Foreword

In 1997, when I was writing the first volume of the book you're now holding, the field of business geographics was just beginning to explode. Fast and affordable personal computers were by then widespread throughout the private sector. Developers of GIS technology like ESRI were seeing wider adoption of their new easy-to-use "desktop mapping" software programs (like ArcView® GIS and Atlas GIS™) in the business world. The earliest applications focused on mapping things like store locations, customers, and competitors. This evolved into geodemographics, the thematic display of socioeconomic data organized by such small-area geographies as ZIP Codes and census tracts. Reliable geospatial data—the crucial geographically referenced information that populates a GIS database—was at the time also becoming more widely available through a burgeoning cottage industry of commercial providers, and an unbelievable volume of free data was beginning to surface on the Internet. The book we published, *ArcView GIS Means Business,* was a snapshot in time that documented some of the creative and profitable GIS applications of a dozen firms.

Now, five years later, as we take another snapshot of the business geographics landscape, much has changed. For one thing, the Internet has played a much larger and more important role than most people would have thought possible in '97. Web-based map- and direction-finding sites are hit millions of times daily, and most corporate Web sites include links to some sort of direction-finding or mapping functionality. The Internet suddenly makes it possible for businesses to reliably and securely deliver their increasingly sophisticated GIS applications, maps, and data from central servers to far-flung employees and customers anywhere on the planet. The Internet has also enabled the creation of huge spatial data libraries, many linked directly to the actual data source. ESRI's Geography Network℠ includes direct links to thousands of GIS data sets as well as metadata (information *about* the data itself). An interconnected web of spatial data now exists to describe virtually every nook and cranny of the planet— literally a *digital earth*—and GIS is the vehicle that navigates its surface (and depths).

Just as networks and hardware have improved dramatically in the past five years, so has GIS software. As a result, business geographics has grown well beyond the basic desktop-mapping functions that spawned it. For a tenth of what it would have cost a business less than a decade ago (and *if* someone could be found to do it), savvy businesses today now do what I call *geoanalysis*. The days of simply displaying data thematically are gone. Today, the latest geoanalytic software allows one to actually analyze the relationships between the location of things and events to create *new* information, such as determining a delivery driver's optimal route through a congested urban area, or modeling the spatial dynamics of demand among grocery stores in a highly competitive market.

Sometimes this new information is used internally to increase efficiency and thereby save money. But increasingly, the new information can also be packaged and sold as a new product or service. In this way, GIS and geospatial technologies have become major driving forces in the emerging networked global economy.

Of course, people are behind all this progress. There is a growing body of GIS professionals working in the private sector, constantly pushing the envelope and delivering spatially enabled applications to their constituents, customers, or employees. Upper management is beginning to appreciate the edge that can come from analyzing and understanding the spatial dynamics

of their firms. There is also a growing trend toward offering GIS training in business schools. Independent developers and consultants are building GIS applications tailored to the specific needs of the retail, commercial, and residential real estate, marketing, health care, manufacturing, and transportation industries. Not surprisingly, just as the rest of the world has been catching up to the West in the use of computers and the Internet, so too has the international business community been rapidly adopting and adapting GIS into its own markets and industries.

Business geographics is no passing fad, as the stories in this new collection attest. The fundamental significance of location in the operation of any business cannot be overstated. In the next five years, as more and more bright people focus their attention on the business opportunities offered by geospatial technology, I predict we will see an explosion of imagination and innovation that will dwarf the one documented in this volume. Geography matters in business; it always has.

Christian Harder
Redlands, California
March 2002

Introduction

Geographic information systems (GIS) continue to change the landscape of the business world. Once the tool of geographers and cartographers, GIS has moved from the research center to the corporate cubicle, from the scientist's workstation to the businessman's personal computer, from the mapmaker to the manager. In the process, it has grown into a multibillion-dollar industry employing tens of thousands of people.

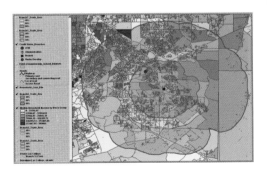

GIS at work

Business managers, marketing strategists, financial analysts, and professional planners increasingly rely on GIS to organize, analyze, and present their business data. By tying information to specific locations, such as street addresses, ZIP Codes, and census tracts, they are creating "business maps" that help them identify patterns and understand relationships not apparent from tables and charts.

Whether they're scouting store locations, reorganizing sales territories, improving delivery routes, identifying new markets, or publishing maps on the Internet, these "spatially literate" users have learned to unleash the power of GIS in their businesses.

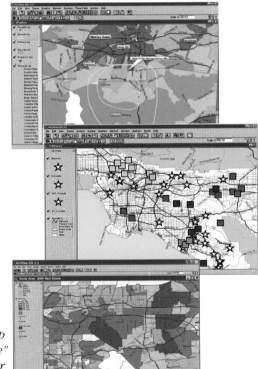

GIS-generated maps like these help businesses of all kinds better "see" their operations, make smarter decisions, and boost profits.

Why geography matters

To many people, geography is a tangle of dusty facts, like *The capital of New Zealand is Wellington* or *Death Valley has the lowest elevation in the Western Hemisphere*. Unless one is a game show contestant, it's hard to see the relevance of these tidbits of information. But suppose somebody wants to sell you a roadside diner in the Mojave Desert. Are you interested? If you know that the diner is located on Interstate 15—the main thoroughfare between Southern California and Las Vegas—you just might be. If, on the other hand, it lies on a forsaken stretch of highway in the Sheep Hole Mountains, you'd tell the seller to take a hike. It's in this sense—knowing where things are as an essential element to rational decision making—that geography matters to business.

Fine—but isn't this just plain common sense? After all, it doesn't take a genius to put a hamburger stand next to a high school or a bait shop by a lake. But things aren't always that simple. Consider a couple of examples:

After studying population and economic growth in the western United States, an airline adds direct flights to a handful of new cities and sees its numbers fly.

In Texas, a department store, analyzing credit card receipts by ZIP Code, infers that a large number of its customers drive along a particular section of freeway to reach the mall—so the store makes some smart choices about where to place billboard ads.

In cases like these, the business decisions are not at all obvious. What is clear, though, is that geographical considerations shaped the outcome.

Linking location to information (or bringing the *where* to bear on the *what*) is a process that applies to many aspects of business. Choosing a site, targeting a market, planning a distribution network or delivery route, drawing up sales territories, allocating resources—all these problems involve questions of geography. Where are my customers—actual and potential?

In which neighborhoods or ZIP Code areas do consumers with the right profile live? Where will they be living five years from now? Where are my competitors located? Which areas might be underserved?

Sometimes the questions are large in scope, and sometimes they're quite specific: How close is the nearest freeway exit? How far away is the airport or the waterfront? Which buildings are properly zoned, have affordable leases, and lie within a five-minute walk of the subway station?

GIS provides the power to answer these and many other questions quickly, accurately, and demonstrably. And that, in short, is what makes it such a valuable tool to business.

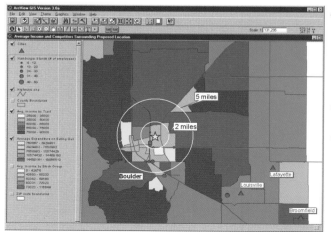

A fast-food franchisor uses GIS to analyze a possible new site (marked with a yellow star). Relevant factors include the average age and income of people in the surrounding area, the locations of major roads, and the proximity of competitors.

What is GIS?

What is a geographic information system? There are probably as many definitions as there are applications for GIS. For the purposes of this book, a GIS is a particular kind of software program that runs on personal and network computers. In many ways it resembles a database program (it analyzes and relates information stored as records), but with one crucial difference: each record in a GIS database contains information used to draw a geometric shape—usually a point, a line, or a polygon.

That shape, in turn, represents a unique place on earth to which the data corresponds. In other words, a record in a GIS file describing Travis County, Texas, would include not only fields of text and numeric information (name, area, and so on), but also fields of spatial data enabling the computer to draw Travis County as a boundary of a certain size and shape. You can therefore think of a GIS as a spatial database—a database that stores the location and shape of information.

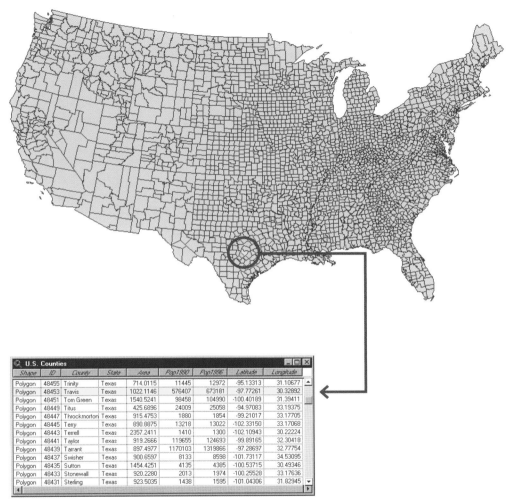

Shape	ID	County	State	Area	Pop1990	Pop1996	Latitude	Longitude
Polygon	48455	Trinity	Texas	714.0115	11445	12972	-95.13313	31.10677
Polygon	48453	Travis	Texas	1022.1146	576407	673181	-97.77261	30.32892
Polygon	48451	Tom Green	Texas	1540.5241	98458	104990	-100.40189	31.39411
Polygon	48449	Titus	Texas	425.6896	24009	25058	-94.97083	33.19375
Polygon	48447	Throckmorton	Texas	915.4753	1880	1854	-99.21017	33.17705
Polygon	48445	Terry	Texas	890.8875	13218	13022	-102.33150	33.17068
Polygon	48443	Terrell	Texas	2357.2411	1410	1300	-102.10943	30.22224
Polygon	48441	Taylor	Texas	919.2666	119655	124693	-99.89165	32.30418
Polygon	48439	Tarrant	Texas	897.4977	1170103	1319866	-97.28697	32.77754
Polygon	48437	Swisher	Texas	900.6597	8133	8598	-101.73117	34.53095
Polygon	48435	Sulton	Texas	1454.4251	4135	4385	-100.53715	30.49346
Polygon	48433	Stonewall	Texas	920.2280	2013	1974	-100.25528	33.17636
Polygon	48431	Sterling	Texas	923.5035	1438	1595	-101.04306	31.82945

Each record in this map file contains spatial information needed to draw a particular U.S. county. When the file is opened, the computer draws a complete county map of the United States.

But a GIS doesn't simply store and display information about places or physical features, it also stores and displays information that can be linked to places—that is, information that has a geographical location. And, as it happens, that encompasses a great deal of information. The fact that two plus two equals four has nothing to do with geography (although it would if it were true in some places and false in others). On the other hand, the fact that luxury cars are mostly bought by people who earn more than $100,000 a year does have a geographical aspect. So does the fact that a significant percentage of Hispanic people prefer to buy groceries with Spanish-language labeling or to shop in a store where Spanish is spoken. A GIS can show where that is.

For this reason, a GIS is more than a computer system for drawing maps (although it does draw maps extremely well). It's really a system for mapping and analyzing the geographical distribution of data. And the data is any information that can be stored in a database, so long as it can be linked to a location.

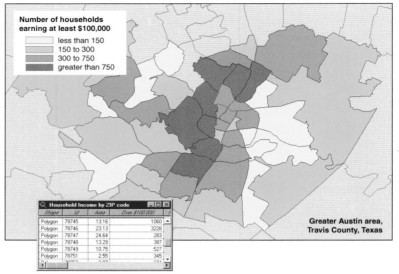

This map of household income in Travis County, Texas, shows the ZIP Codes with the most people earning over $100,000 a year. A luxury car dealer could target these ZIP Codes for marketing efforts.

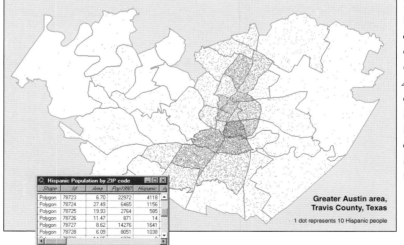

This dot density map of the same area shows concentrations of Hispanics. A supermarket chain catering to this segment of the population could use the map to help locate a new store.

GIS map files can represent the whole world or any part of it, in greater or lesser detail, by any of various subdivisions (political boundaries, postal codes, census designations, streets, and so on). They can represent all kinds of natural and man-made features as well: rivers, lakes, highways, hospitals, and so on. These map files are available from a variety of sources. Many come included with GIS packages; others can be obtained from both commercial vendors and government agencies. In addition, map files can be created from data (such as a customer address list) that is implicitly geographic. There are map files to represent almost any place with almost any kind of statistical information a person might want. And because a GIS is a relational database, existing data can be easily linked to an appropriate map file.

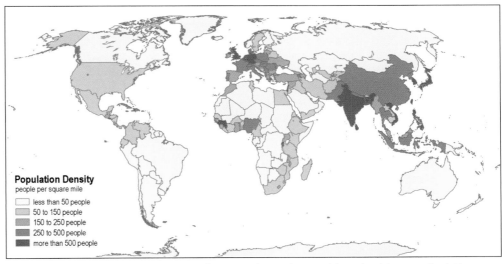

Population Density
people per square mile

less than 50 people
50 to 150 people
150 to 250 people
250 to 500 people
more than 500 people

A GIS map can represent an area as large as the entire world, as in this map depicting population density by country.

Assessed value

Under $100,000
$100,000 to $125,000
$125,000 to $150,000
$150,000 to $200,000
Over $200,000

Or, a map can show an area as small as a neighborhood. This map displays the property values of land parcels in a section of San Jose, California.

The map paradigm

We often say "I see" to mean "I understand." Pattern recognition is something human beings excel at—that's why we know a Great Dane and a French poodle are both dogs, despite their obvious differences, and that's why human scrutiny is still the best way to analyze satellite and aerial reconnaissance photos in an era of massive supercomputing capability.

One of the great insights of GIS is that there is a vast difference between seeing data in a table of rows and columns (a display mode natural to computers and accountants) and seeing it presented in the form of a map. The difference is not simply aesthetic, it's conceptual—it turns out that the way we see data has a profound effect on the connections we make and the conclusions drawn from it.

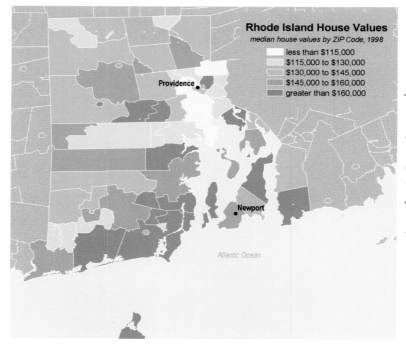

Zip	Pop 1996	Post Office	Median home value
02861	26129	PAWTUCKET	111900
02863	17163	CENTRAL FALLS	102900
02864	28595	CUMBERLAND	143200
02865	14407	LINCOLN	156700
02871	16437	PORTSMOUTH	173300
02872	121	PRUDENCE ISLAND	156000
02874	3637	SAUNDERSTOWN	169500
02877	1139	SLOCUM	162800
02878	13745	TIVERTON	139600
02879	14374	WAKEFIELD	161500
02881	7565	KINGSTON	172300
02882	14383	NARRAGANSETT	168200
02883	1837	PEACE DALE	116800
02885	11462	WARREN	138100
02886	40875	WARWICK	116400
02888	20794	WARWICK	114500
02889	20702	WARWICK	114000
02891	21610	WESTERLY	155800
02892	4300	WEST KINGSTON	150500
02893	28126	WEST WARWICK	124300
02894	743	WOOD RIVER JUNCT	124200
02895	38452	WOONSOCKET	127300

Rhode Island House Values
median house values by ZIP Code, 1998

- less than $115,000
- $115,000 to $130,000
- $130,000 to $145,000
- $145,000 to $160,000
- greater than $160,000

The table and the map both show the same data: the median value of homes by ZIP Code in Rhode Island. But even for someone familiar with the state's geography, the table has limited value as a tool for understanding the housing market. By contrast, the information on the map is easy to grasp, even for a person who's never been to Rhode Island.

GIS helps users visualize data

A GIS lets a user visually represent the data in any field of a map file: as differing shades of color, as symbols of different sizes, as dot patterns of varying density, or in other ways. If the information in the file is changed, the display is automatically updated. And if the user has different map files representing features that occupy common geographic space, multiple layers of data can be added to the same display. This lets the user create a map as rich in information as the data will allow.

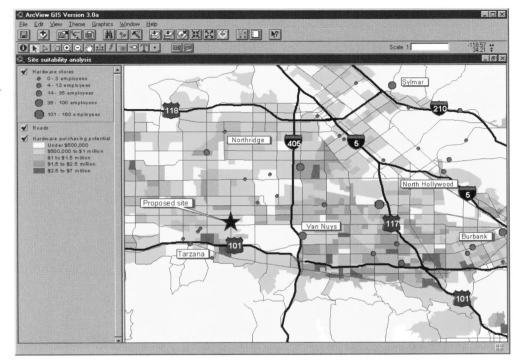

This map of the area around Van Nuys, California, contains multiple layers of spatial data, each from a separate data file. The entire area is shaded yellow to red according to consumer purchasing power. City streets are shown as thin gray lines, while highways and interstates are thicker purple lines. Pink dots represent the locations of retail hardware stores; the size of each dot reflects the number of employees the store has. All the information in the map is relevant to a specific business issue: where to locate a new hardware store.

GIS helps analyze data

As with any database, the greatest virtue of a GIS is its analytical power. A GIS has a full array of query tools: logical operators, math functions, a scripting language. The ability to display the results of your queries geographically is an advantage in itself, but GIS offers something much more important—the unique capacity to do spatial analysis, making it possible to ask and answer questions that are beyond the scope of traditional databases.

Suppose a business owner has three stores and wants to compare the demographics around each to help understand why two are thriving and one is performing poorly. Using spatial analysis, the owner can calculate a demographic profile for all the households that lie within a fifteen-minute drive of each store.

Or say an owner wants to make sure her delivery driver is taking the most efficient route as he makes rounds. With spatial analysis the owner can find the best route from the factory and give the driver turn-by-turn directions.

In the examples above, the maps are certainly useful, but it is the *information extracted* by spatial analysis that is most important. This information would either be impossible or extremely difficult to obtain without a GIS.

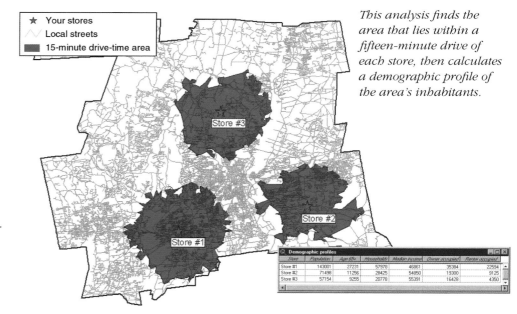

This analysis finds the area that lies within a fifteen-minute drive of each store, then calculates a demographic profile of the area's inhabitants.

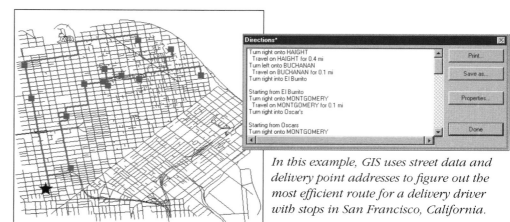

In this example, GIS uses street data and delivery point addresses to figure out the most efficient route for a delivery driver with stops in San Francisco, California.

GIS and the Internet

On the Internet, interactive applications allow customers to produce their own custom maps, twenty-four hours a day, anywhere in the world. Whether it's in helping people find the nearest automated teller machine, or showing a traveler all the Chinese restaurants within a mile of her hotel, maps delivered via the Internet are already changing the way businesses think of customer service.

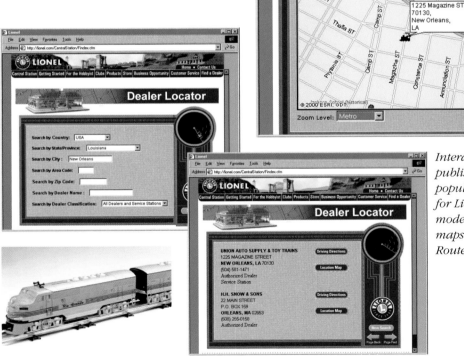

Interactive maps are increasingly published on the Internet, like this popular dealer locator developed for Lionel, famous maker of model trains. The user-friendly maps are made possible by ESRI's RouteMAP™ IMS software.

Case studies and GIS

The case studies in this book illustrate a range of GIS problem-solving methods and data from a variety of sources. The common thread is software produced by ESRI, the world's largest company fully dedicated to GIS.

GIS for business solutions is one of the company's cornerstones; the product line is used throughout the world, helping businesses make better decisions, save money, and improve customer service.

The appendix at the end of this book goes into greater detail about the variety of business-related resources available from ESRI and others. The case studies that now follow are intended to provide insight into what GIS means to businesses and business-oriented activities in a host of varied locales.

ESRI's Web site, www.esri.com, provides numerous pages about the company and its range of GIS products.

In the retail world, the difference between success and failure often comes down to one key element: picking the right location. But finding that perfect spot isn't always easy. Intelligent decision making is the sum of knowing who one's customers are and where they live, work, and travel. In a world where many retailers go out of business within a few years of opening their doors, the consequences of picking the wrong location are more than sobering.

That's why GIS is playing such a vital role with one of the United States' major commercial real estate enterprises—a company where "location, location, location" is being honed to a technologically fine art. Company officials say the application is saving time and money for both itself and its clients.

Expanding a portfolio

Edens & Avant is one of the fastest growing commercial real estate firms in the United States, with assets valued at $1.9 billion. Based in South Carolina, the company has served the eastern U.S. for nearly thirty-five years, and it has home and regional offices in nine states and the District of Columbia. The company owns, operates, and develops Necessity Retail® Centers and leases space to national and regional retailers. Edens & Avant's current portfolio comprises more than 250 shopping centers in eighteen states.

The company also provides a full complement of corporate and third-party commercial real estate services, including commercial brokerage, office and industrial leasing and management, health care, retail leasing and management, and development. More and more, Edens & Avant is using GIS to satisfy the demands of retailers and other clients who want the best information—as soon as possible—to help select a location that will make their businesses work and let profits flow.

Edens & Avant has its home office in Columbia, South Carolina, and twelve regional offices across the eastern United States. The company operates its grocery-anchored Necessity Retail Centers over a wide region.

Using interactive search tools

In the past, retailers looking for a new site often had to wade through mountains of folders, paperwork, fold-out maps, and tables of statistical and demographic information. Now, E&A OnSite, a GIS-based tool, links retailers to Edens & Avant shopping centers that best meet their site location needs. From the Necessity Retail Centers page on the company's Web site, users can search by center name, state, or metropolitan statistical area, or do demographic searches of a given area, using factors such as population, number of households, and household income. Customers simply enter their specific location and demographic criteria, and, within seconds, a list of suitable shopping centers in the Edens & Avant retail centers portfolio is generated.

ESRI® ArcView Business Analyst and *Route*MAP IMS software were used to develop E&A OnSite.

Edens & Avant's Web site, www.edensandavant.com, is the starting point for quick navigation to GIS-based retail site location services.

Searching by name

Here, searching by center name, information on the Buckeye Plaza in Cleveland, Ohio, is displayed. Users find a wealth of facts, including a property description, summary of local demographics, and a contact name for leasing information. A printable site plan is displayed, which provides names and locations of other retailers in the shopping center, and an interactive map shows the particular site location in different geographic contexts.

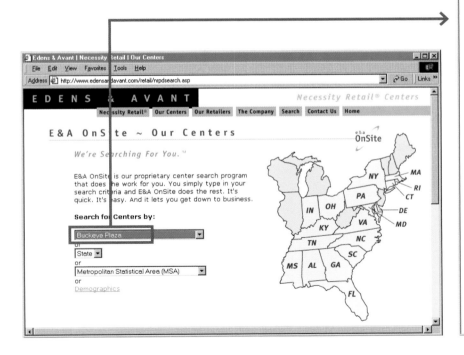

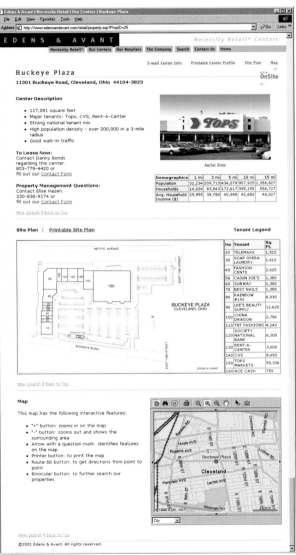

Searching by state

Here, searching by state (in this case, Florida) leads to an interactive map of the state, and a listing of more than a dozen shopping centers. Each is linked to more detailed information. For example, clicking on Promenades Mall in Port Charlotte reveals its specific data, site plan drawing, and interactive map.

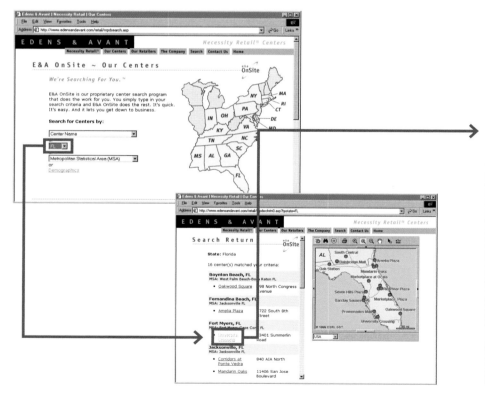

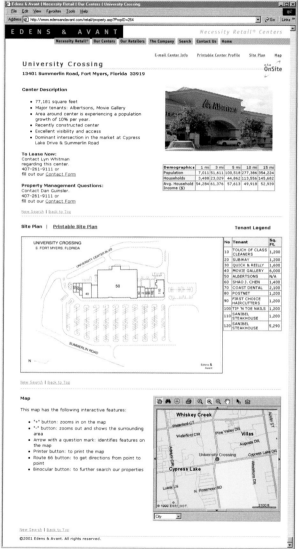

Searching by metro area

Searching by Metropolitan Statistical Area (MSA) is another way to make E&A OnSite find a prime location. In this case, clicking on Atlanta among the many MSAs leads to several attractive retail locations in that part of Georgia. Clicking on one of the shopping center names from the listing provides information on a center in Smyrna.

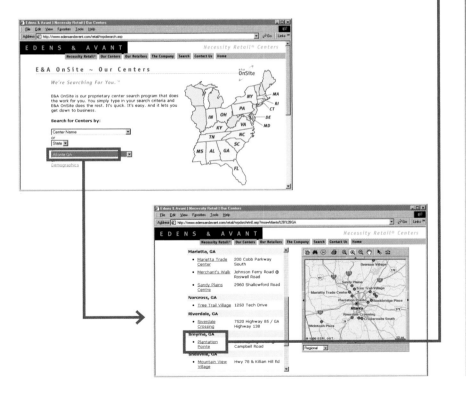

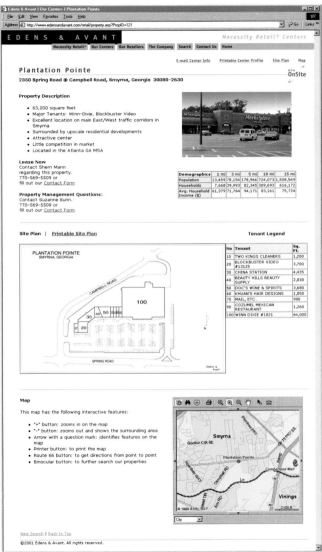

Another way to search

Here, with E&A OnSite's Demographic Search mode, a search of all states is launched, with demographic information limited to a one-mile radius. The user wants to search areas with populations of 25,000 to 50,000, households numbering from 8,000 to 20,000, and average household incomes between $30,000 and $75,000. The results include two shopping centers that fit the retailer's requirements: one center in Boston, the other in Cleveland. The full story of South Bay Center in Boston is told in the screen on the far right: data, description, lease contact, site plan, photo, and map location.

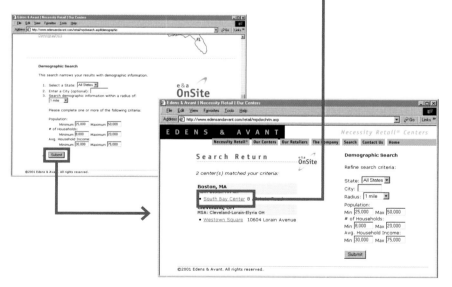

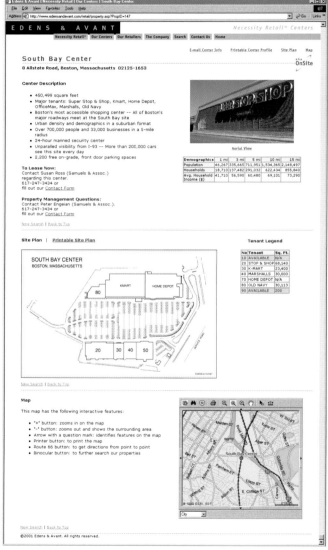

A client gets help

One of the first clients to use Edens & Avant's OnSite tool was Check Into Cash, Inc., a financial services company headquartered in Cleveland, Tennessee. The firm was interested in opening a new store in North Carolina, primarily the area near the city of Albemarle. Using E&A OnSite while in consultation with Edens & Avant representatives, Check Into Cash quickly found the location it wanted in Albemarle's First Street Station shopping center, and Edens & Avant turned empty space into leased space.

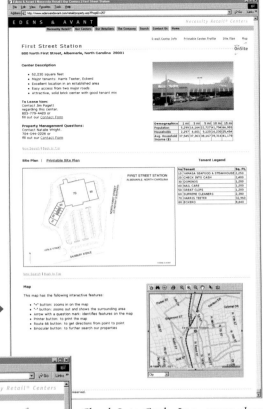

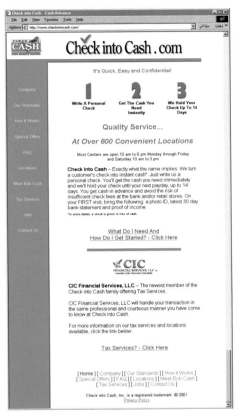

Check Into Cash, Inc., www.checkintocash.com, used Edens & Avant's GIS-based site location services to open a new store in North Carolina.

A variety of uses

GIS is the technology for building the data, providing the analysis, and distributing the knowledge about issues that involve location. For this reason, GIS at Edens & Avant is used in many ways and involves every department of the company in some fashion. Maps and analyses are performed for presentations to retailers, investors, and decision makers.

The development group uses GIS to study new markets for potential development. Competition locations around the new development are entered, allowing an experienced developer to draw the trade area for a potential development by viewing competition, population density, and any other spatial factors. Trade area demographics are produced that aid the decision-making process. If it looks as though the population dictates the need for a new shopping center, then the demographics can be used to determine which tenant mix best fits the population.

Developers use thematic maps as part of the equation in determining the primary and secondary trade areas for a new shopping center.

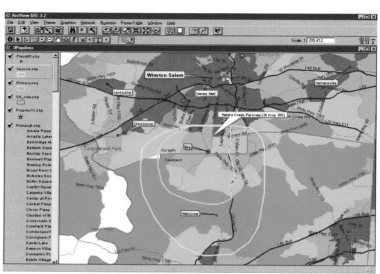

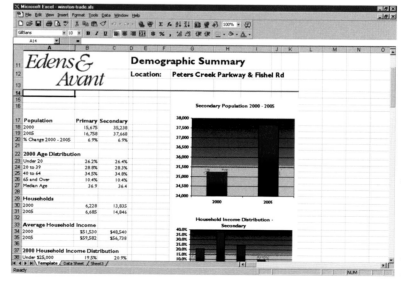

A Microsoft® Excel spreadsheet shows the demographics of the primary and secondary trade areas for a proposed shopping center.

A multitude of benefits

The retail leasing group at Edens & Avant uses GIS to communicate with prospective and existing retailers on market conditions, growth possibilities, and competition factors. The maps and statistics derived from GIS help to show a prospective tenant reasons for setting up shop at a particular location. This is done by mapping out the competitive retailers in the area in relationship to high-population areas and other demographic attributes.

Using GIS for spatial analysis helps Edens & Avant to understand its existing markets as well as evaluate new ones for development or acquisition. By combining the expertise of its employees with GIS, Edens & Avant has the ability to leverage information technology better now than at any other time in the company's history.

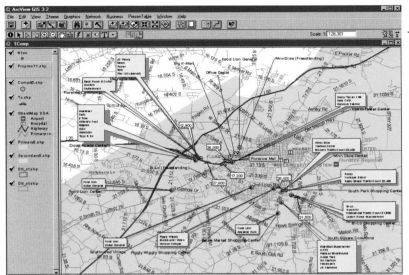

Market plans for the shopping centers include thematic maps, traffic counts, and locations of retailers, as well as the anchor and center trade areas for the shopping center.

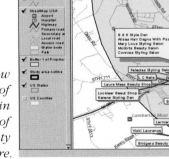

GIS is used to show the locations of beauty shops within a five-mile radius of a proposed beauty supply store.

Return on investment

Company officials say that while it's sometimes difficult to calculate the return on investment regarding expenditures for technology, there is concrete evidence that going to an interactive system using computers, GIS, and the Internet saves money. Because clients can view information about Edens & Avant's centers online, the costly production of printed brochures is eliminated. It's also easier to update information and keep it current, and Edens & Avant's employees can essentially print out their own marketing materials from anywhere with an Internet connection.

Clients also reap benefits. In the past, it could take weeks for clients to compile lists of retail centers, geocode locations, and produce demographics. Today, this type of analysis takes just seconds, saving valuable time and money.

The system

Dell® 410 Precision Workstation; Dell Power Edge 4300; Microsoft® Windows® NT® 4 and IIS4; ArcView Business Analyst; *Route*MAP IMS.

The data

*Route*MAP IMS comes with the U.S. street data and landmark data from Geographic Data Technology, Inc. ArcView Business Analyst comes with the demographic data from CACI Marketing Systems Group (acquired in early 2002 by ESRI). Edens & Avant provides its proprietary portfolio GIS layer, with MSA and state centroids derived from National Transportation Atlas Database (NTAD) data for 1999.

Acknowledgments

Thanks to David Z. Beitz of Edens & Avant, and Ed Ryan of Check Into Cash.

Delivering seafood smartly

Retail deliveries often have to be fast, and nowhere is this requirement more important than in the perishable foods industry. And if the perishable commodity is fresh fish, the stakes are even higher. For distributors in this highly competitive industry, getting fresh fish to restaurants and grocery stores just when the customer needs it is critical.

One such firm is showing how GIS-based delivery systems are vastly superior to the old way of doing business. Loading docks are saner places than before; warehouse workers are loading trucks more systematically; fewer mistakes are being made; and drivers are able to start deliveries earlier and make all their stops while traveling fewer miles.

A big name in seafood

Morey's Seafood International LLC is one of the largest fresh fish and seafood distributors in the United States. According to company legend, it all started the day the founder traded a pickup truck full of corn for a truck full of fresh fish that had broken down in his hometown of Motley, Minnesota. The year was 1937. In the decades since then, Morey's line of smoked and prepared seafood products have been sold all across the United States. The company also delivers thousands of pounds of fresh fish daily to restaurants and stores in a number of U.S. regions. In fall 2000, Morey's began using GIS to improve the delivery of its products in the Detroit area, one of the firm's biggest markets.

Morey's Seafood International, headquartered in Minneapolis, has a number of manufacturing and distribution facilities throughout the Midwest and Southwest. On the Web, its site is www.moreys.com.

Old gives way to new

Morey's Detroit facility trucks fresh and frozen fish and smoked fish products on a daily basis to grocery stores and restaurants. For years, trucks were loaded and deliveries were made the old-fashioned way: drivers typically showed up for work all at the same time, even though there was a limited number of dock doors for loading; the loading dock area was often chaotic, with workers trying to get more than two dozen vehicles loaded at only four docks. On top of that, fixed-zone routing was used to make deliveries. That's where truck routes are assigned to specific geographic areas, and orders are assigned to vehicles depending on their fixed routes.

The system was less than efficient. One zone in a delivery area could get overloaded with orders, while the zone next to it might have only a few orders. After receiving their delivery orders, drivers would decide their own stop-and-deliver sequences—often having to reorganize the products on their trucks. Sales personnel, who often are the folks most answerable to the clients, might know the sequence of deliveries but could only guess at the times when deliveries would be made.

Morey's officials decided that a GIS solution was needed to improve the situation, and Truck Dispatching Innovations, based in Chicago, used ESRI software to help.

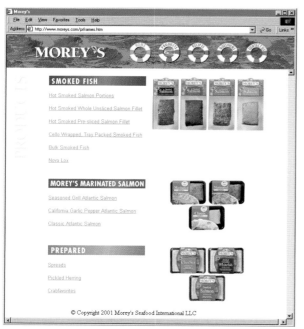

Truck Dispatching Innovations, www.tdinnovations.com, is the consulting firm using ESRI's ArcLogistics™ Route software to streamline Morey's delivery system in Detroit.

Importing orders and reviewing data

For Morey's, the route-streamlining process starts by using GIS software to load vital information into the computer and organize it; this includes the names and addresses of the company's clients, start and stop times for delivery trucks, the number of minutes it takes to make a delivery, and weights of products to be trucked and dropped off.

With a GIS, the information also can be more easily checked for completeness and accuracy. Dispatchers make a special point of looking at the "comment" columns, because sales personnel occasionally may add special requests to change a customer's delivery time or make other modifications relating to an order.

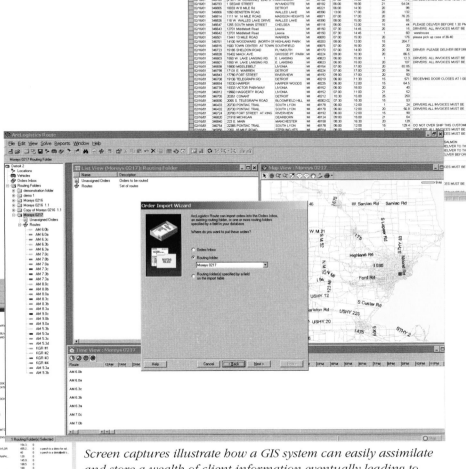

Screen captures illustrate how a GIS system can easily assimilate and store a wealth of client information eventually leading to better routing and improved deliveries.

Creating routes

Next comes the task of configuring the routes. First, the dispatcher confirms that the proper number of delivery trucks are available and in place for the day, and that start and stop times for each vehicle are properly assigned. Meanwhile, unassigned orders can be seen in a map view as black dots. Having the orders geographically displayed is important; in the past, dispatchers had to look through stacks of paper to assess whether certain orders were next to each other geographically or spread farther apart. Then, when certain data is checked and accounted for, the dispatcher can simply click on a "build route" icon and generate optimal routes and schedules.

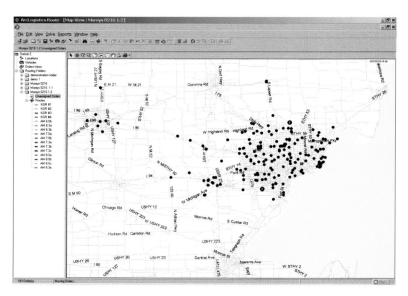

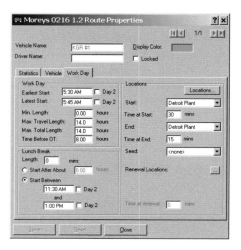

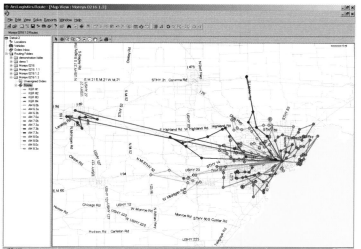

These screen captures illustrate and are among the steps a Morey's dispatcher uses to check and assign vehicles, confirm orders, and build custom routes to accommodate a day's deliveries of fish. Black dots on the map at top represent unassigned orders. Colored lines and dots on the other map represent routes.

The GIS calculates each vehicle's time windows, load capacity, available hours, and other factors in creating optimal routes. If need be, the dispatcher can also easily tweak a computer-generated route and make adjustments. By simply clicking and dragging on the computer screen, an order from one route can be transferred to another.

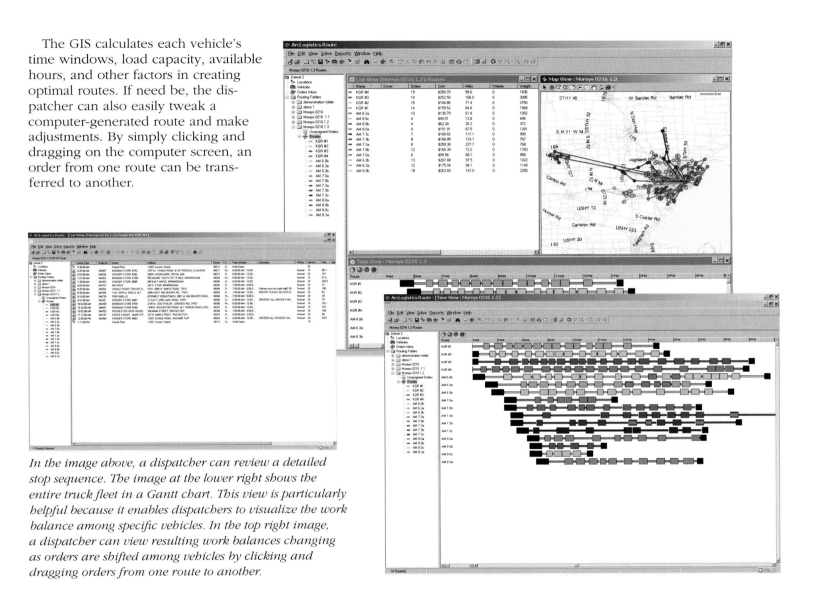

In the image above, a dispatcher can review a detailed stop sequence. The image at the lower right shows the entire truck fleet in a Gantt chart. This view is particularly helpful because it enables dispatchers to visualize the work balance among specific vehicles. In the top right image, a dispatcher can view resulting work balances changing as orders are shifted among vehicles by clicking and dragging orders from one route to another.

Maps and output reports

Many of the GIS-generated reports can be customized. Drivers receive overview maps of their routes and route manifests that detail the sequence of stops, the estimated times of delivery, delivery comments, and other pertinent information. If required, the software can produce detailed written directions from each stop to the next, plus detailed maps of the local vicinity.

Loading dock personnel are provided load reports that detail the stop and delivery sequences so trucks can be loaded with the last stop's products in the "nose" or front of the truck, and the first stop's load right by the door. Improved loading saves time for delivery drivers.

Company administrators and managers find manager summaries and dispatching summaries useful in seeing an overview of route costs, mileage, and how trucks' carrying capacities are being used, among other considerations.

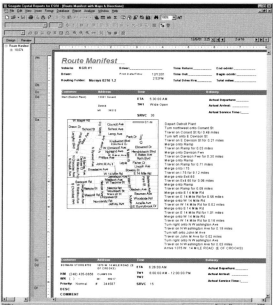

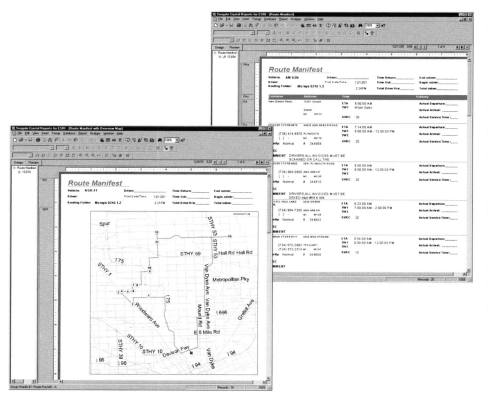

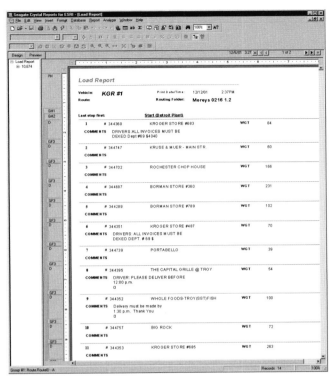

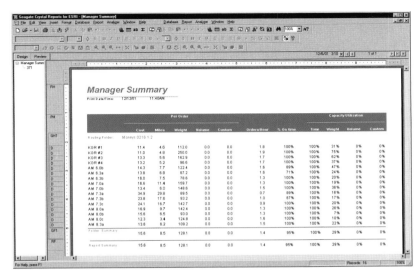

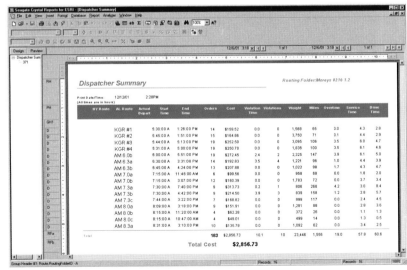

A variety of maps, route manifests, and summary reports can be generated with a GIS to assist warehouse personnel, truck drivers, dispatchers, and managers.

Saner docks

After the GIS was put in place, the 8-to-10-A.M. madhouse on the loading dock—trying to get more than two dozen trucks loaded through four dock doors—calmed down considerably. With ArcLogistics Route, trucks could be more evenly scheduled, and more drivers could get on their way earlier, beating traffic and allowing more time for deliveries. Reducing chaos on the dock also helped to eliminate loading mistakes.

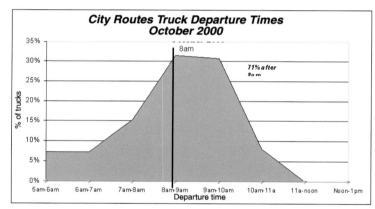

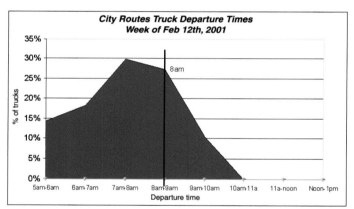

These charts, prepared by Truck Dispatching Innovations, show how GIS software helped Morey's manage its truck routing more effectively. Prior to the improvements, 71 percent of the trucks were leaving after 8 A.M., with a huge bulk of them leaving between 8 and 10 A.M. After the improvements, only 37 percent of the fleet was leaving after 8 A.M.

Optimizing loads

In the first six months of using ArcLogistics Route, the average load per vehicle increased more than 30 percent—from nine orders per route to more than twelve. Morey's local delivery fleet of twenty-eight trucks was reduced to twenty-three, an 18 percent decrease. Loading fewer trucks more efficiently led to a significant reduction in transportation costs.

Interestingly, the dip seen in January resulted after a veteran warehouse dispatcher left the firm; within a couple of weeks, the dispatching function was back at full efficiency and orders-per-route improvements continued to show the progressive rise that began after use of ArcLogistics Route started in December.

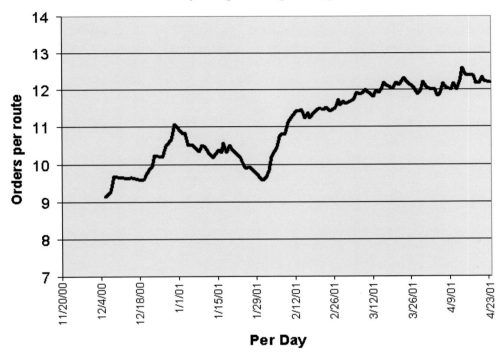

Detroit average orders per route by day
(10 day moving average)

Research and information tracking by Truck Dispatching Innovations helped show Morey's managers the improvements made by using GIS technology.

Maps show the difference

Nothing illustrates the positive changes for Morey's Detroit area product routing better than these maps showing the "before and after." Prior to using GIS, much of the routing tended to be "back and forth" driving, with trucks heading out from the warehouse along certain pathways to make deliveries, then driving back along the same route or in the same general direction to the warehouse to begin new out-and-back patterns. After GIS streamlined the routes, circular patterns emerged, and deliveries were made more economically.

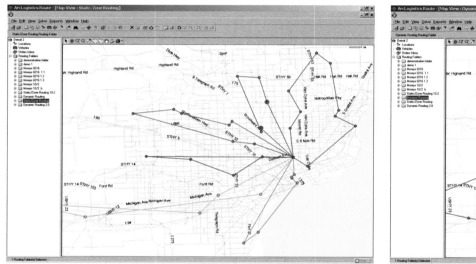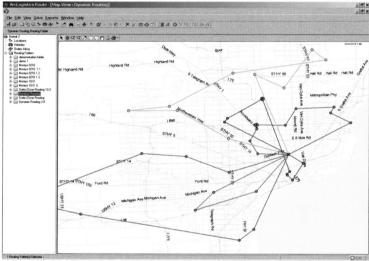

The map at the left shows routing patterns before GIS was used to streamline and reconfigure the routes, as illustrated by the map at the right.

Keeping track of drivers

ArcLogistics Route also helps Morey's in other ways. Maps and information developed with it can be meshed with GPS (Global Positioning System) data, and Morey's dispatchers can audit their trucks' actual travel compared to the planned routes. It's a way to help ensure that drivers are on track and doing their jobs. The system also enables dispatchers to e-mail orders, instructions, and other information to drivers, as changes may develop through the day. Drivers can also directly update the real-time status of orders and deliveries, such as whether they are pending, skipped for some reason, or completed.

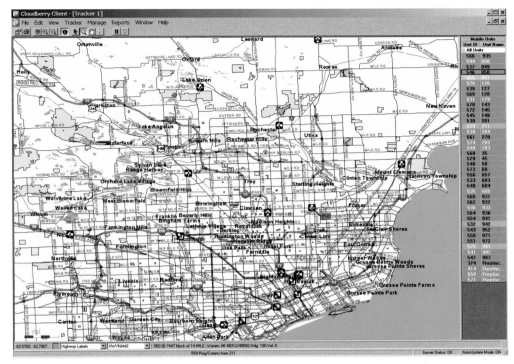

This map of the Detroit area uses icons with directional arrows to show the locations and driving directions of Morey's delivery trucks. It shows how GIS and GPS technologies can be combined to help dispatchers, minute to minute, manage the company's fleet more effectively. The system uses Internet-based Cloudberry™ AVL (automatic vehicle tracking) technology. Routes are generated with ArcLogistics Route, then easily exported to Cloudberry and placed in its system as another layer of information for reference.

The map below shows how GIS and GPS technologies help a dispatcher track a Morey's driver on another route in Detroit. The wide, light green line represents the established route. The thin red line is the driver's actual route.

The vehicle starts at the Morey's facility on the bottom right and, after some off-route traveling, makes a stop. Then the driver heads east and does stops 18 and 19 (these were scheduled as his last two stops), before heading west and getting back on the route. It appears the driver skipped stops 7 and 8. The tracking system is set to transmit every fifteen minutes, so most likely the driver was able to deliver at stops 7 and 8 before the next fifteen-minute transmittal. Later the driver takes an easterly route instead of the more northern route indicated by the computer map. At the top the driver again takes an unscheduled detour.

The detours and out-of-sequence deliveries don't automatically mean drivers are inattentive or not doing their jobs properly. The changes could be due to traffic problems or communications with the dispatcher. But the technology does give dispatchers and managers a way to see how drivers are handling their routes, in case problems or issues need to be resolved. This is another example of GIS helping businesses operate more effectively.

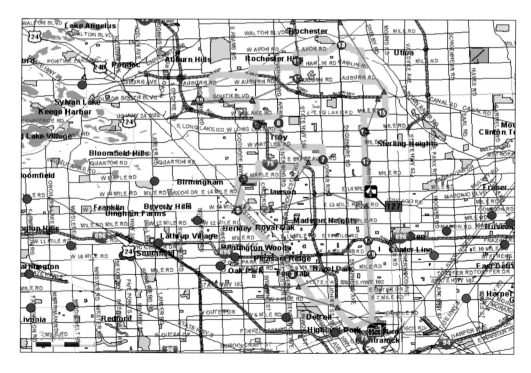

The software

ESRI ArcLogistics Route and AVL/GPS by Cloudberry from Air-Trak.com, Inc.

The data

GDT Dynamap/2000®, and customer data from Morey's Seafood International.

Acknowledgments

Thanks to Michelle M. Pape at Morey's Seafood International, John Handler at Truck Dispatching Innovations, Chris Walz at RouteSmart Technologies, Inc., and Karl Terrey at ESRI.

The reinsurance industry is an often complicated business, but in simple terms it involves insurance for insurance companies. Every year, primary insurers are walloped by billion-dollar natural catastrophes—earthquakes, volcanoes, hurricanes, tornadoes, floods—not to mention the havoc caused by man-made accidents and terrorism. The losses are staggering, often beyond the means of any one insurance company to pay off all its claims using just its own resources. That's where reinsurers come in—large companies standing securely in the background, stepping in to help pay off losses sustained by their partnered insurance companies, who themselves have paid premiums to the reinsurers. The mega-losses are then shared and paid out, and everybody stays in business.

It's a basic principle repeated throughout the industry, and it involves insurance and reinsurance in its many forms: catastrophe, property, agriculture, casualty, and credit and surety, among others.

Today, some reinsurers, including Munich Re and Swiss Re, are using GIS in various ways, including the invention of products and services that assist their insurance partners and educate the public at large.

The world's biggest

Münchener Rückversicherungs-Gesellschaft, also known as Münchener Rück or Munich Re, has its headquarters in Munich, Germany, and is the largest reinsurance firm in the world. Its more than five thousand clients are spread across 150 countries, and the firm employs more than five thousand people around the globe. Munich Re made a name for itself early on by successfully paying off millions of dollars in losses after San Francisco's "Great Quake" in 1906, an earthquake and fire of devastating proportions. Today, the company continues to lead the way in reinsurance as it relates to natural disasters, and GIS technology is part of this ever-developing story.

Munich Re, founded in Germany in 1880, today has a well-developed Web presence at www.munichre.com, with pages of information on its history, corporate structure, and range of insurance products and services, among other features.

Natural hazards explained

Using ESRI ArcInfo™ software and other resources, Munich Re developed a CD–ROM called "World of Natural Hazards," an interactive collection of information on earthquakes, volcanoes, floods, and other natural disasters. Digital techniques provide users with simple and quick methods of identifying hazards within seconds. Produced in both German and English, the CD–ROM, which is purchased through Munich Re, is intended primarily for insurance specialists, engineers, and anybody with a professional or private interest in the subject of natural hazards.

The CD–ROM includes a modular world map showing where natural disasters occur, with a comprehensive list of locations that can be analyzed, and specific information about the types of natural hazards affecting any location chosen. It includes scientific information on hazards; a glossary of geoscientific and insurance terminology; scales and measuring tools for understanding degrees of natural hazards; a worldwide catalog of catastrophes; and a country-by-country database with statistics and an overview of relevant natural hazards. The CD–ROM is also a launching point to consultancy and other services provided by Munich Re's Geo Risks Research Department.

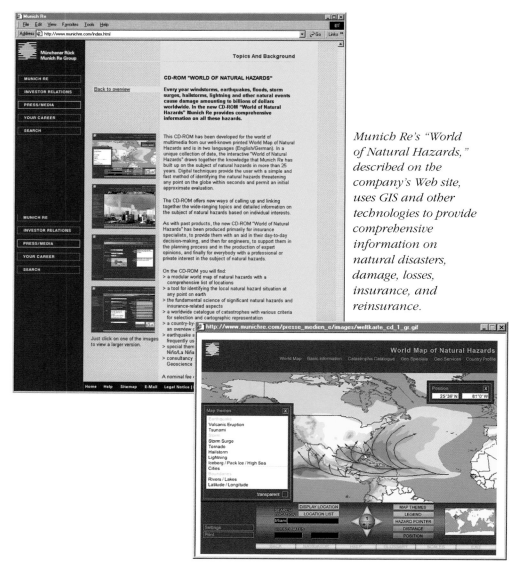

Munich Re's "World of Natural Hazards," described on the company's Web site, uses GIS and other technologies to provide comprehensive information on natural disasters, damage, losses, insurance, and reinsurance.

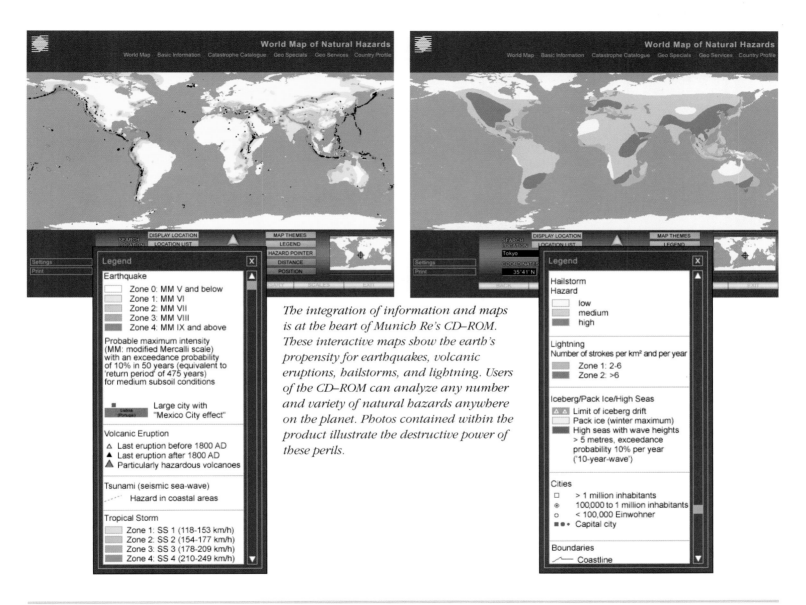

The integration of information and maps is at the heart of Munich Re's CD–ROM. These interactive maps show the earth's propensity for earthquakes, volcanic eruptions, hailstorms, and lightning. Users of the CD–ROM can analyze any number and variety of natural hazards anywhere on the planet. Photos contained within the product illustrate the destructive power of these perils.

One country's natural hazards

Let's say an insurance specialist needs quick information on Japan, a country and land mass known for its earthquakes, volcanoes, and tsunamis, the giant waves created by earthquakes. Munich Re's CD–ROM allows the agent to quickly bring up maps of the country, along with charts, tables, and other data screens.

Clicking on the Country Profile heading and navigating to Japan, the user is led to an information-packed profile that includes six subheadings: Geography, Government, Demography, Economy, Transportation, and Natural Hazards. Clicking on each leads to detailed summaries of helpful data and information. For example, the Geography summary provides specific country location; land area; a breakdown on how much of the country is land and water, respectively; coastline length; climate and terrain; and land use.

The Demography summary provides information on various aspects of population, including raw totals, growth, and densities. The Natural Hazards summary contains color-coded bar charts that show the degree of exposure to various natural hazards and the percentages of the country affected by those conditions, including earthquakes, volcanic eruptions, tsunamis, storms, tornadoes, hailstorms, flood, drought, and frost.

From left to right: Demography summary, Geography summary, Natural Hazards summary.

Maps and spatial views

The CD–ROM's map-producing abilities tell underwriters and other users even more about specific natural threats. It's a quick navigation from the world map and location list to a zoomed-in map of Japan, which shows the locations and types of earthquake zones, patterns and places of volcanic eruptions, and coastal zones where tsunamis are prone to hit hardest.

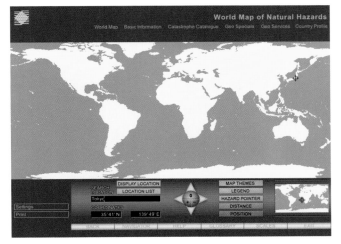

Maps and data tell a serious story about potential damage from earthquakes and tsunamis, but photos included with the CD–ROM are worth a thousand words. An earthquake in Kobe, Japan, in 1995 set off destructive fires; a tsunami that hit a Japanese island two years earlier did widespread damage on one side of the island's southern tip.

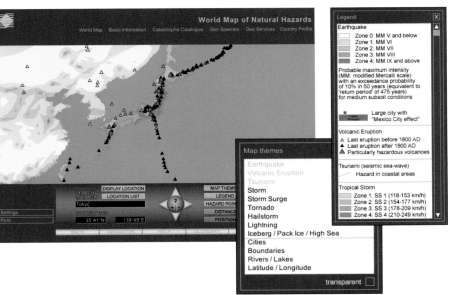

Hazards elsewhere

Volcanoes, earthquakes, and tsunamis threaten property worldwide. Munich Re's CD–ROM lets users explore, study, and analyze the Mediterranean region as easily as anywhere else on the planet. The map on this page highlights the volcanic threat and history of eruptions in Italy, as well as severe earthquake zones in Turkey. Broken red lines identify coastal zones where flooding could occur after large earthquakes. Clicking on the Scales heading on the CD–ROM program lets a user see and learn more about tsunamis and coastal zone flooding.

This map shows major regional zones where lightning tends to strike with greatest frequency and proximity. Clicking on the CD–ROM's Glossary heading lets users navigate to alphabetized explanations of various natural perils; in this case, "L" leads to "lightning."

Measuring the harms

Clicking on the Scales heading leads to interactive windstorm scales that measure the relative effects of wind on structures, buildings, and objects. In the example on this page, winds at zero on the Beaufort Scale (a method of assessing strengths of air movements) indicate calm. At 4 on the scale, air movement strength is a moderate breeze, and at 10, a violent storm causing damage. Knowing what degrees of wind tend to hit where on the planet—and the consequences, damage, and losses that result—helps those in the insurance industry make better-informed decisions that benefit both insurer and insured.

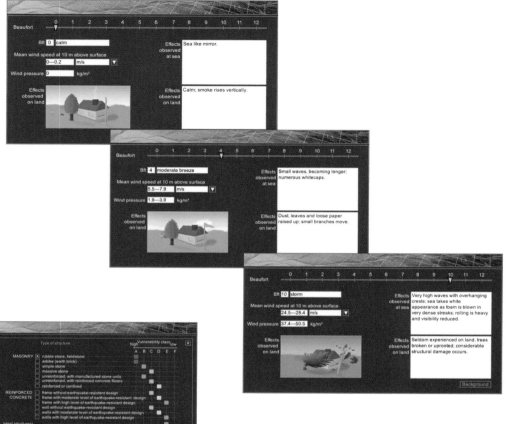

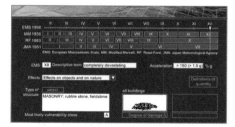

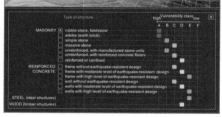

Interactive tools describing and illustrating earthquake scales help underwriters know how quakes of different magnitudes will damage structures, depending on what those structures are made of.

Climate changes and hazards

Clicking on the Geo Specials heading leads to an interactive treasure trove of information and maps on climate change, global warming, and El Niño and La Niña, the periodic warming and cooling of the Pacific Ocean surface waters near the equator—and some of the destructive natural hazards that result.

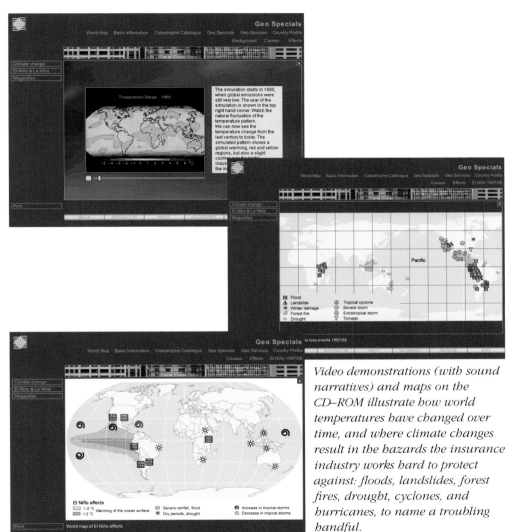

La Niña-related Hurricane Mitch hammered Honduras in 1998. The CD–ROM charts show that flooding dominated as an El Niño–La Niña hazard in 1997–98, while forest fires (resulting in part from hot weather and drought) accounted for the greatest degree of loss.

Video demonstrations (with sound narratives) and maps on the CD–ROM illustrate how world temperatures have changed over time, and where climate changes result in the hazards the insurance industry works hard to protect against: floods, landslides, forest fires, drought, cyclones, and hurricanes, to name a troubling handful.

NATHAN is online

Munich Re also has NATHAN ("NATural Hazards Assessment Network") up and running on the company's intranet. Developed with ESRI's ArcIMS® software, the new online function is being planned for public accessibility on Munich Re's Internet site in autumn 2002. NATHAN provides some of the same information afforded by its CD–ROM, but also offers additional services for underwriters and others needing information on natural hazard risk assessment and management. NATHAN links users in real time to Munich Re's global data warehouse.

The software

ESRI ArcInfo 8.01 (Workstation, ArcGrid™, ArcCatalog™, ArcMap™, ArcToolbox™); Macromedia® FreeHand™; Apple® QuickTime®; MAPublisher®; Adobe® Illustrator®; ESRI ArcIMS (for NATHAN).

CD–ROM system requirements

200-MHz-minimum PC running Microsoft Windows® 95, Windows 98, Windows 2000, or Windows NT; 64 MB RAM (128 MB recommended); monitor resolution 800 × 600 at 66,536 colors (true color recommended); 8-speed CD–ROM drive.

Apple Macintosh® PowerPC® running Mac® OS 8.5 or higher; 64 MB RAM (128 MB virtual); monitor resolution 800 × 600 at 66,536 colors (true color recommended); 8-speed CD–ROM drive.

The data

Bureau of Meteorology, Melbourne, Australia; Canadian Space Agency, Saint-Hubert, Canada; Central Intelligence Agency (CIA), Washington, D.C.; Deutsches Klimarechenzentrum, Hamburg, Germany; Deutsches Zentrum für Luft- und Raumfahrt e.V., Oberpfaffenhofen, Germany; Dinnes, D., Munich; Deutsch Presse-Agentur GmbH, Frankfurt am Main, Germany; Earthquake Engineering Research Institute (EERI), Oakland, California; ESRI, Redlands, California; Fletcher, J. E., National Geographic Society, Washington, D.C.; Hydro-Quebec, Canada; Instituto Geofisico, Escuela Politécnica Nacional, Quito, Ecuador; National Oceanic and Atmospheric Administration (NOAA), Washington, D.C.; South African Weather Bureau, Pretoria, South Africa; Steinwachs, M., Hanover, Germany; The Institute of London Underwriters, London, England; U.S. Geological Survey, United States.

Acknowledgments

Thanks to Jürgen Schimetschek and Andreas Siebert of Munich Re, and Lee Burton of ESRI.

One of the first

Swiss Reinsurance Company, also known as Swiss Re, was founded in Zurich, Switzerland, in 1863. Today, after nearly 140 years of doing business, it is also one of the largest reinsurance firms in the world, with approximately five thousand clients in a hundred countries. The company employs about nine thousand people, and it has more than seventy offices in thirty countries around the globe. Swiss Re, which was founded in the wake of a devastating fire in the Swiss town of Glarus in 1861, enhanced its already growing reputation in 1906 by paying off millions in losses (as did Munich Re) after San Francisco's disastrous earthquake and fire. Today, the company is a world leader in reinsurance and is using GIS technology to provide online services.

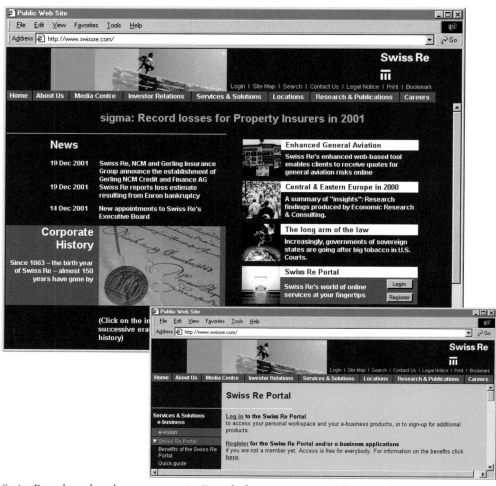

Swiss Re, whose headquarters are in Zurich, has numerous Web pages (www.swissre.com) devoted to its history, organization, corporate philosophy, and wide range of insurance products and services. The Swiss Re Portal is the gateway to the company's extensive offering of online services.

Natural perils and CatNet

Using ESRI's ArcIMS software, Swiss Re developed "CatNet," an online mapping and data service for interactive exploration of information on earthquakes, volcanoes, storms, floods, tornadoes, and other natural disasters. Users can instantly access country-specific information for locations all over the earth.

Available in English, CatNet services are provided to Swiss Re clients free of charge. All others can take advantage of an eight-week free trial period before registration, at which time an annual fee is charged. The service is intended for underwriters and other insurance and reinsurance specialists and professionals, as well as general Internet users and other decision makers with an interest in the field.

CatNet includes a hazard atlas with a variety of maps that show where natural disasters occur, as well as concise, country-by-country lists of geographic and economic data, insurance penetration and loss potentials, information tables, a glossary, and links to many other insurance and reinsurance contacts, including carriers and regulatory agencies. Further, CatNet also directs users to Swiss Re's Client Services department.

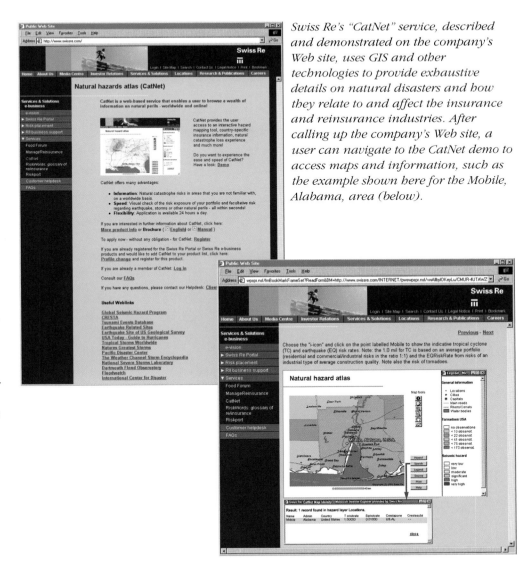

Swiss Re's "CatNet" service, described and demonstrated on the company's Web site, uses GIS and other technologies to provide exhaustive details on natural disasters and how they relate to and affect the insurance and reinsurance industries. After calling up the company's Web site, a user can navigate to the CatNet demo to access maps and information, such as the example shown here for the Mobile, Alabama, area (below).

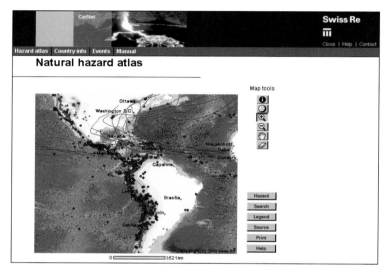

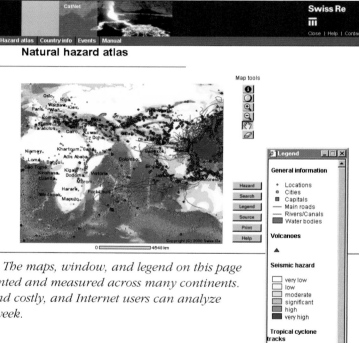

Interactive maps and data are the key components of Swiss Re's CatNet. The maps, window, and legend on this page show how specific hazards can be identified first as to type, then pinpointed and measured across many continents. The system helps explain where natural perils make life most difficult and costly, and Internet users can analyze different countries and regions twenty-four hours a day, seven days a week.

Hazards in New Zealand

If an underwriter needs maps and data for New Zealand, a click on "Country info" starts the search, producing a page with a table of contents as well as a simple map. Clicking on headings within the table leads to concisely written explanations of insurance facts and terms, along with charts that provide information about events and economic data, insurance penetration and loss potential. Clicking on the simple map takes the user to the detailed map on the next page.

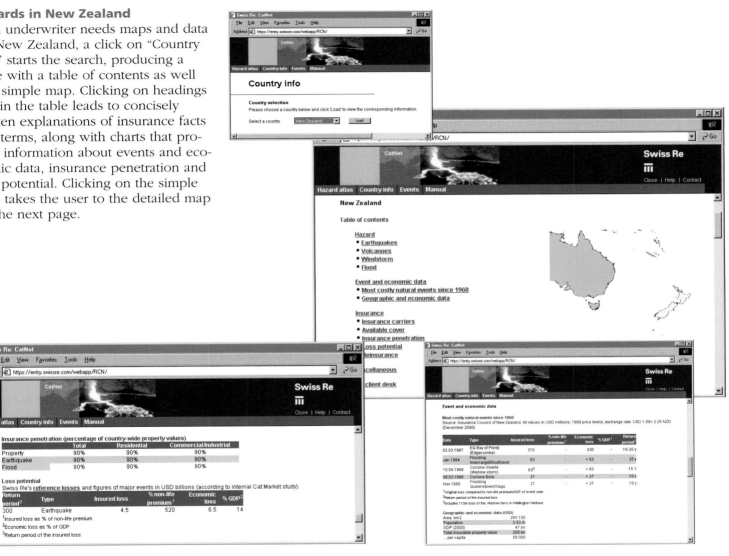

Maps, layers, legends

CatNet's mapping functions help insurers and others quickly access even more about particular natural hazards. Navigating from the simple map on the previous page, or from the world map shown earlier, takes the user to more fully developed maps that show specific natural threats. Here, for example, a general map of New Zealand can be instantly modified with any of a number of map layers. Clicking on "Hazards" leads to a window containing the names of a number of map layers. Clicking the "Seismic hazard," "Earthquake epicenters," "Volcanoes," and "Tropical cyclone tracks" boxes produces a color map of the island nation; clicking on "Legend" produces a legend that shows where the natural perils exist or occur, and with what gravity.

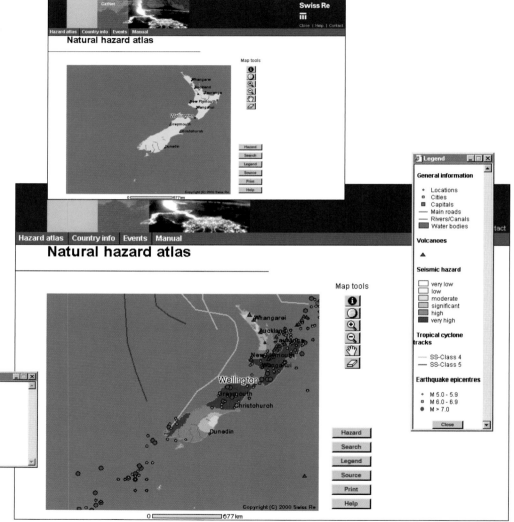

Perils elsewhere

Mexico is another place plagued by natural disasters, and CatNet's maps, data, tables, and other resources explain what they are, where they occur, and what damage they can do. The map and legend on this page show where earthquakes, seismic activity, volcanoes, and high winds are threats. By using the "identify" tool, detailed information from the database will be displayed for each individual hazard feature.

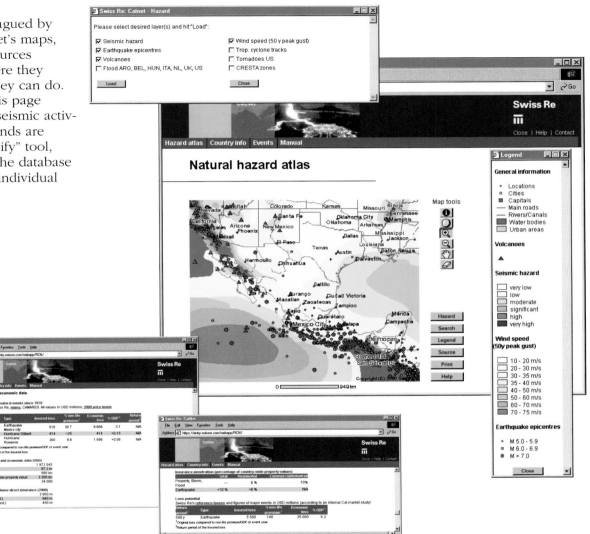

Using one of CatNet's search functions, a user can track and find more specific information about different kinds of disasters. As illustrated here, typing in "Gilbert" and clicking on the appropriate layer heading (in this case, "Tropical cyclone tracks") produces a map showing where Hurricane Gilbert swept through parts of Mexico and a wide region beyond in 1988. In another example, typing in "Mexico City" and clicking on the "Earthquake epicenters" layer produces a map showing where a highly destructive quake hit in 1985.

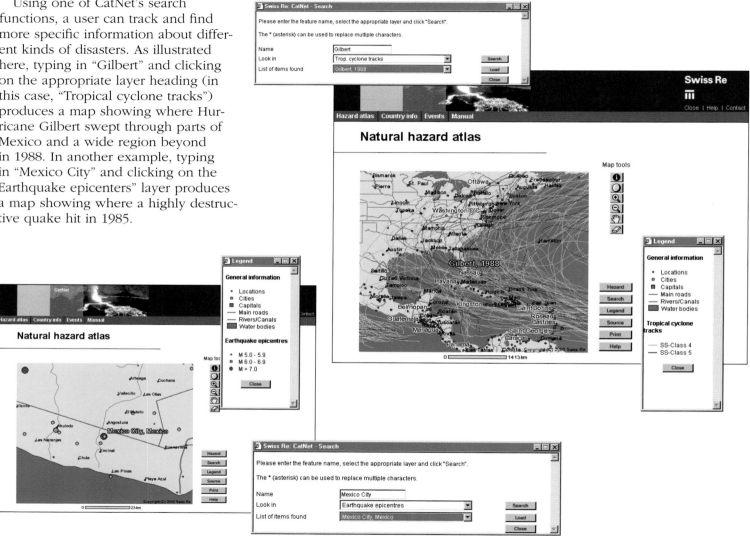

More about events

CatNet's "Events" heading provides a list of catastrophic events: the forty most costly insurance loss events from 1970 to 2000; the forty most severe catastrophes during the thirty-year period; the twenty most costly insurance loss events in 2000; and the twenty most devastating catastrophes in 2000. CatNet's "Manual" heading not only leads to a downloadable and detailed set of instructions on how to use CatNet, but also features links to a number of Web sites with additional information on perils, losses, insurance, reinsurance, and GIS.

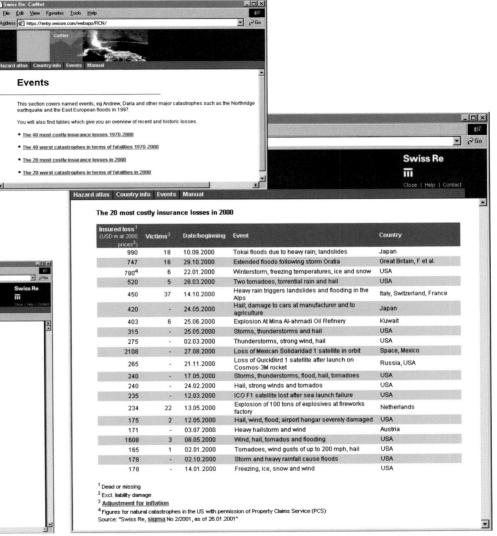

The 20 most costly insurance losses in 2000

Insured loss[1] (USD m at 2000 prices[2])	Victims[3]	Date/beginning	Event	Country
990	18	10.09.2000	Tokai floods due to heavy rain; landslides	Japan
747	16	29.10.2000	Extended floods following storm Oratia	Great Britain, F et al.
780[4]	6	22.01.2000	Winterstorm, freezing temperatures, ice and snow	USA
520	5	28.03.2000	Two tornadoes, torrential rain and hail	USA
450	37	14.10.2000	Heavy rain triggers landslides and flooding in the Alps	Italy, Switzerland, France
420	-	24.05.2000	Hail; damage to cars at manufacturer and to agriculture	Japan
403	6	25.06.2000	Explosion At Mina Al-ahmadi Oil Refinery	Kuwait
315	-	25.05.2000	Storms, thunderstorms and hail	USA
275	-	02.03.2000	Thunderstorms, strong wind, hail	USA
2108	-	27.08.2000	Loss of Mexican Solidaridad 1 satellite in orbit	Space, Mexico
265	-	21.11.2000	Loss of QuickBird 1 satellite after launch on Cosmos-3M rocket	Russia, USA
240	-	17.05.2000	Storms, thunderstorms, flood, hail, tornadoes	USA
240	-	24.02.2000	Hail, strong winds and tornadoes	USA
235	-	12.03.2000	ICO F1 satellite lost after sea launch failure	USA
234	22	13.05.2000	Explosion of 100 tons of explosives at fireworks factory	Netherlands
175	2	12.05.2000	Hail, wind, flood; airport hangar severely damaged	USA
171	-	03.07.2000	Heavy hailstorm and wind	Austria
1608	3	08.05.2000	Wind, hail, tornados and flooding	USA
165	1	02.01.2000	Tornadoes, wind gusts of up to 200 mph, hail	USA
178	-	02.10.2000	Storm and heavy rainfall cause floods	USA
178	-	14.01.2000	Freezing, ice, snow and wind	USA

[1] Dead or missing
[2] Excl. liability damage
[3] Adjustment for inflation
[4] Figures for natural catastrophes in the US with permission of Property Claims Service (PCS)
Source: "Swiss Re, sigma No 2/2001, as of 26.01.2001"

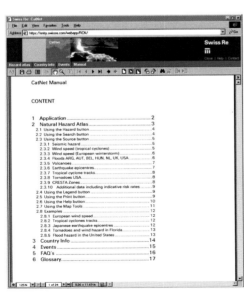

Easy access online

Users who want to try out CatNet can go to www.swissre.com/portal and register either as guests or full clients. After completing online registration forms, they are guided to CatNet and many other online services.

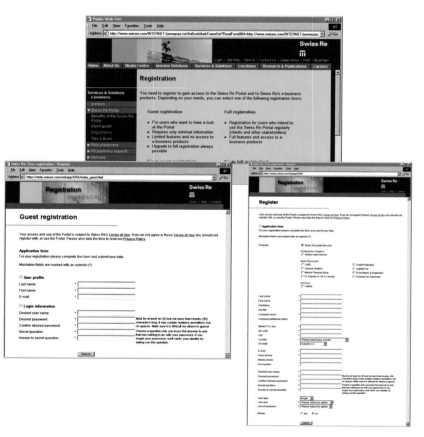

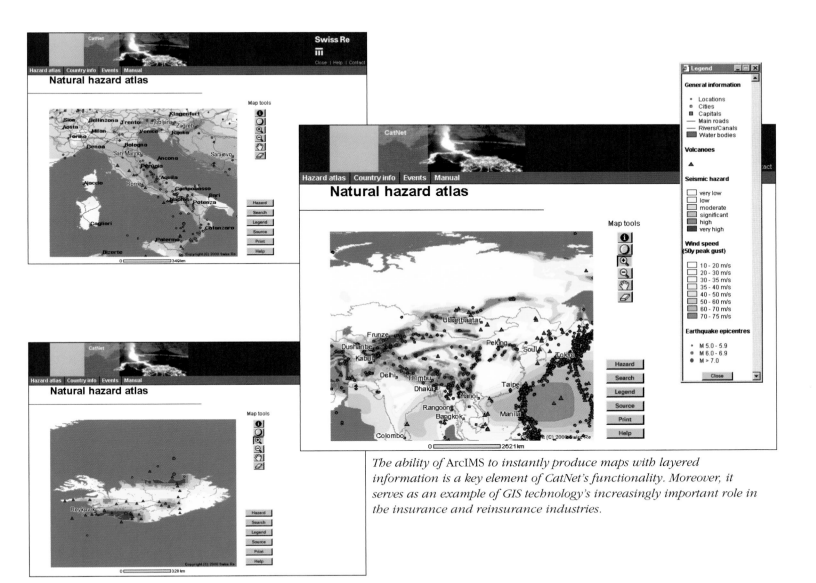

The ability of ArcIMS *to instantly produce maps with layered information is a key element of CatNet's functionality. Moreover, it serves as an example of GIS technology's increasingly important role in the insurance and reinsurance industries.*

The system

Sun™ E-450 server running ESRI ArcIMS, Oracle®, and Apache software.

The data

Various data sources, including Global Seismic Hazard Assessment Program (GSHAP), Unisys® (tropical cyclone tracks), EUROWIND and EQECAT (wind speed), Federal Emergency Management Agency (FEMA), Global Volcanism Program, Smithsonian Institution, University of Nottingham, Dr. J. C. Doornkamp, U.S. Geological Survey, National Earthquake Information Center, Tornado Project Online, Catastrophe Risk Evaluation and Standardizing Target Accumulations (CRESTA), Infotech Enterprises Europe, Macon AG, Chalk Butte, Inc., and ESRI.

Acknowledgments

Thanks to Cornelia Schmidt of Swiss Reinsurance Company, and Lee Burton of ESRI.

Swiss Re

4

Expanding and growing a credit union

Credit unions, like banks and other savings-related institutions, are a vital part of the world's social and financial fabric. Historically, credit unions typically have been relatively small enterprises serving narrowly defined employment groups within local towns and communities. But today, many credit unions are aggressively widening their geographic reach as they expand their customer base. No longer limiting their memberships to the law officer or the school teacher, the engineer or the machinist, many credit unions are also offering greater and more diverse financial services and amenities, including drive-up lanes, full-service ATMs—even children's play areas in the lobbies. More branch offices are being built, and the decisions about exactly where to open those next branch offices are vitally important.

One such credit union, based in the Lone Star State, is demonstrating how new technologies are spurring this kind of growth, and how GIS and business intelligence are vital to the expansion.

A modest beginning

In 1931, a small group of school-teachers in Dallas, Texas, got together and applied for a credit union charter. And so it began—the Dallas Teachers Credit Union, with initial assets of just sixty-five dollars. For decades the credit union worked hard and grew the old-fashioned way—without the computers, software, and sophisticated databases that eventually became a way of life. Now, with a new name and charter change granted in 2000, the Credit Union of Texas ranks in the top one hundred credit unions in the country in asset size, with $1.3 billion and about 165,000 members. Geographically, the credit union is busting well out of Dallas proper. In recent years its service region has grown from just two counties to an area that now includes all or parts of five counties. It has ten branch offices and eighteen ATMs, with more in the planning stages.

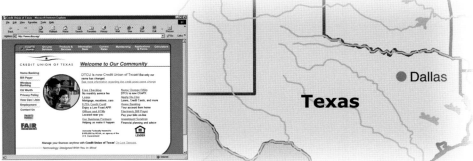

The Credit Union of Texas, formerly known as the Dallas Teachers Credit Union, is headquartered in Dallas, and its Web site is www.cuoftexas.org.

Business intelligence partner

In the late 1990s, the Credit Union of Texas (at that time still known as the Dallas Teachers Credit Union) noticed a trend among its competitors in the Dallas area toward one-to-one marketing: that is, marketing and advertising messages aimed at particular and narrowly defined customers rather than a broadly spread base of "everybody in the area." The credit union also saw that the industry was moving away from occupational-based credit unions catering solely to specific employment groups, to community-based banking that included people holding various types of jobs. The credit union also recognized a new challenge emerging in the community from old rivals: large banks. So, a search began to find technology solutions that could help the Credit Union of Texas become more competitive and vigorous in attracting new members.

In July 1999, the credit union made the decision to use IBM's Enterprise Performance Suite (EPS). The suite contains hardware, software, and consulting products that enable clients to successfully harvest, manage, and analyze data. These Business Intelligence products from IBM, combined with GIS software from ESRI, led the credit union to a better understanding of its overall business, customers, and competition, which enhanced overall decision making.

IBM's Web page, www.ibm.com/ software/bi, is the starting point for information about Business Intelligence products, such as the ones used by the Credit Union of Texas. IBM's Business Intelligence solutions include Web databases that deploy information to employees, partners, and customers; integrated, easy-to-use tools for building and managing data warehouses; and analysis software for forecasting customer preferences, among other features.

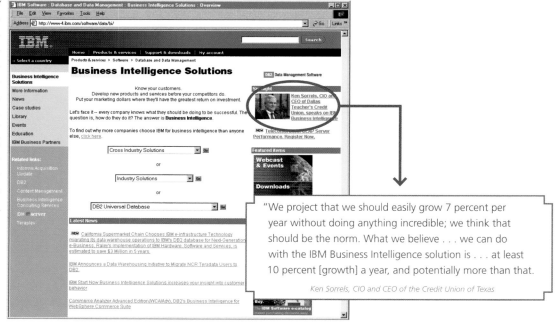

"We project that we should easily grow 7 percent per year without doing anything incredible; we think that should be the norm. What we believe . . . we can do with the IBM Business Intelligence solution is . . . at least 10 percent [growth] a year, and potentially more than that.

Ken Sorrels, CIO and CEO of the Credit Union of Texas

Branch location analysis

Figuring out where to build new branches is extremely important to the credit union. ESRI's ArcView Business Analyst was used to study the trade area of each of the credit union's branches and then used to select new branch and ATM locations. Of particular importance was the need to build new branches to relieve crowding at some of the existing branches. The credit union developed a geographic model that was overlaid on a profitability modeling database of existing customers. The intent was to avoid taking too much business away from existing branches, while identifying new locations that would reduce customer traffic at crowded branches by about 20 percent. The result was the siting of a new branch that resulted in a drain of 22 percent of customers from existing branches.

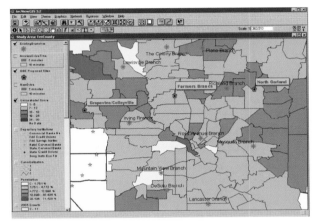

Modeling analysis was conducted to identify potential areas for marketing efforts. The results were then mapped to identify the best locations where customers could be found. The existing branch locations and proposed new branch locations were then overlaid so the credit union could identify the best areas to capture new customers.

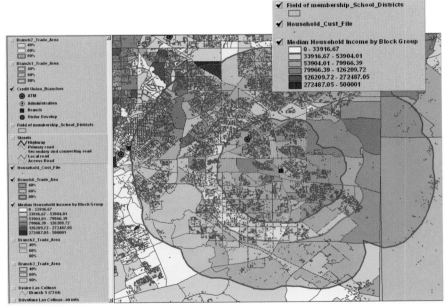

Identifying the trade area—the area where revenue actually comes from—is critical to branch expansion, optimizing profitability, and providing better customer service. Each trade area can be analyzed according to median income, checking account profiles, loans, account balances, products purchased, and profitability. The green area is where 80 percent of one branch's revenue comes from; outer rings show where lesser amounts of revenue are derived.

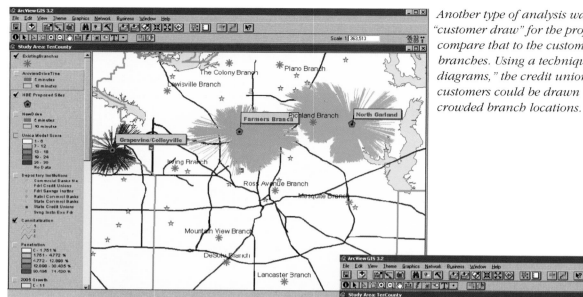

Another type of analysis was performed to identify the "customer draw" for the proposed new branches and compare that to the customer draw from the existing branches. Using a technique that produced "spider diagrams," the credit union was able to identify which customers could be drawn to the new locations from the crowded branch locations.

As an aid in determining new branch locations, an analysis was made of drive times and how far customers were willing to drive to perform certain banking procedures, such as opening a new checking account. It was another way to determine where gaps in the market existed, and logical places to open new branches. Red areas indicate drive times of about five minutes; yellow areas indicate drive times of about ten minutes.

Placing billboard advertising

Mapping branch and ATM locations by use of traffic counts also helped the credit union identify locations for billboard advertising. Identifying streets with lots of traffic was the first step. This was important because the credit union wanted to get the word out about its name change, and it wanted to attract new members to its branches.

The credit union keeps track of its customers' home and work addresses, and it can map out the routes they use in their commutes. This information helps to determine specific locations for billboard advertising and in figuring out what the messages will say. Traffic counts can be overlaid on demographic maps showing areas of high income, number of households, or other features, and all of that analysis helps the credit union fine-tune billboard ad placements and content.

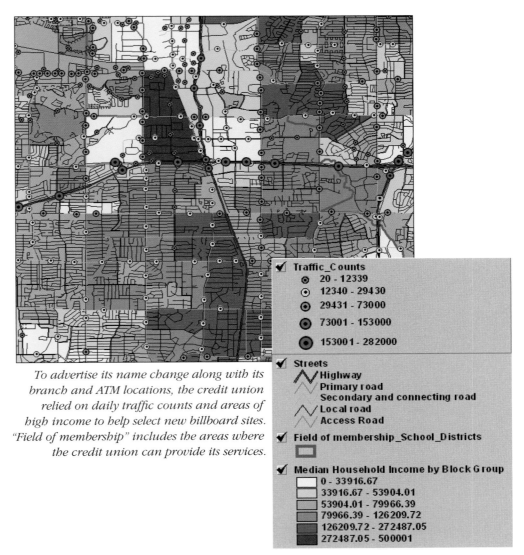

To advertise its name change along with its branch and ATM locations, the credit union relied on daily traffic counts and areas of high income to help select new billboard sites. "Field of membership" includes the areas where the credit union can provide its services.

Traffic_Counts
- ⊙ 20 - 12339
- ⊙ 12340 - 29430
- ⊙ 29431 - 73000
- ⊙ 73001 - 153000
- ⊙ 153001 - 282000

Streets
- /\/ Highway
- /\/ Primary road
- Secondary and connecting road
- /\/ Local road
- /\/ Access Road

Field of membership_School_Districts
- ☐

Median Household Income by Block Group
- ☐ 0 - 33916.67
- 33916.67 - 53904.01
- 53904.01 - 79966.39
- 79966.39 - 126209.72
- 126209.72 - 272487.05
- 272487.05 - 500001

Improving direct marketing

Historically the credit union had sent marketing mail to all of its then 145,000 members, and was happy to get a 1 percent to 2 percent response. This "shotgun" approach was relatively costly and not as effective as credit union officials wished it could be. But with Business Intelligence data and GIS mapping and demographic tools, the credit union could zero in and identify specific profiles of customers for targeted, one-to-one marketing. The result? Mailings to just ten thousand customers—selected by specific economic factors and variables—resulted in response rates of 8 percent to 9 percent. The cost savings were significant and the return on investment was greatly improved.

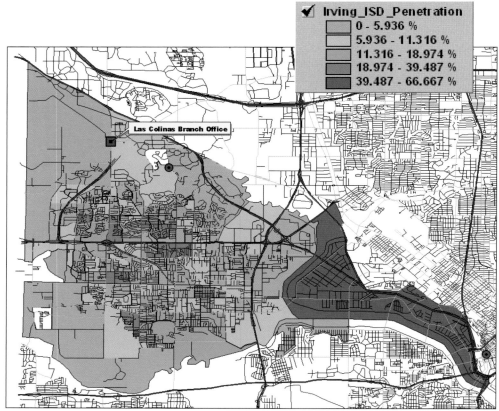

Because the credit union's field of membership is based on school attendance boundaries, these areas became units of GIS analysis. In the Irving Independent School District, for example, the credit union wanted to identify its market penetration. This allowed the credit union to identify specific block groups within the area for target marketing. The red dots indicate locations of ATMs.

From account balance to drive time
Market penetration analyses, keying
on different factors such as account
balances and drive times, help the
credit union determine where to market. These maps, generated with ESRI's
Business Analyst, are examples of
the work product that credit union
officials studied before deciding what
kinds of marketing materials to prepare
and mail.

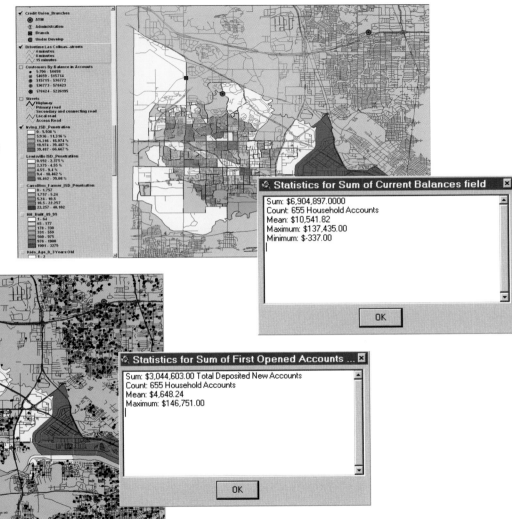

In this example, street file information was overlaid with block group information, and specific areas were identified for target marketing. The number 76 represents the number of households in a block group that match the credit union's profile of a "good" customer. Address ranges were then identified for a mail campaign; the table on this page is a sample of the result. Street segments within this block group were analyzed based on the number of minutes they were from a particular branch. Addresses that were five minutes from the branch were identified, and the credit union used the information for a targeted marketing campaign.

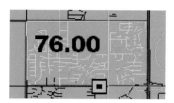

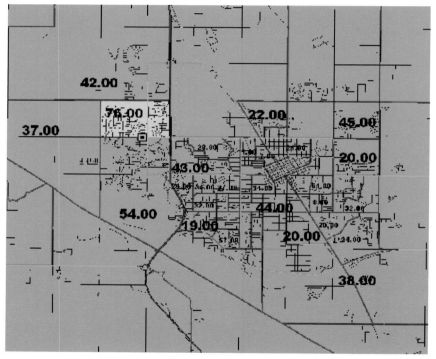

9/11/01   Street Address Ranges By Drive Time From Branch 399, Dallas, Texas

NAME	AREA DI	L_F_ADD	L_T_ADD	R_F_ADI	R_T_ADD	PREFI	ZIPL	CITYL	BRANCH_
	0-5 min								
Abshire	0-5 min	1801	1999	1800	1998		75228	Dallas	399
Abshire	0-5 min	2001	2131	2000	2098		75228	Dallas	399
Abshire	0-5 min	2133	2199	2100	2198		75228	Dallas	399

Expanding the charter

Credit unions are granted charters to operate, and occupation-based charters restrict membership to select employment groups. The Credit Union of Texas, when it operated as the Dallas Teachers Credit Union, was limited to a potential membership base of about 250,000, spread over a roughly two-county region. From that base, the credit union had a membership of about 145,000. When the credit union went to Texas state authorities in 2000 to apply for a new community-based charter, it used ArcView Business Analyst in its presentation.

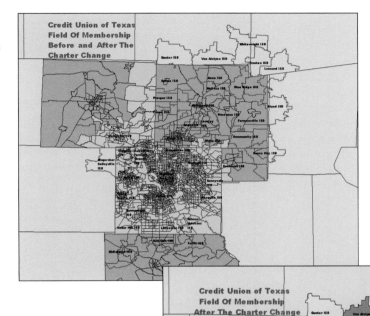

Maps produced with Business Analyst dramatically illustrated for state regulators the credit union's geocoded field of membership and helped show the geographical area served before the charter change (in light green, map at top), and the area it would serve if allowed to change its charter (lower map). Credit union officials say the maps made a tremendous improvement in the power of their presentation to state officials, who ultimately approved the charter change.

Easily finding locations

To enhance the Web site experience for customers, the credit union used ESRI's *Route*MAP IMS to add an interactive mapping function that helps users identify and locate all of its branch and ATM locations. Customers can type in their locations and get driving directions to the nearest branch or ATM machine. These maps complement the standard lists of names and addresses of branch and ATM locations that appear on the credit union's Web pages.

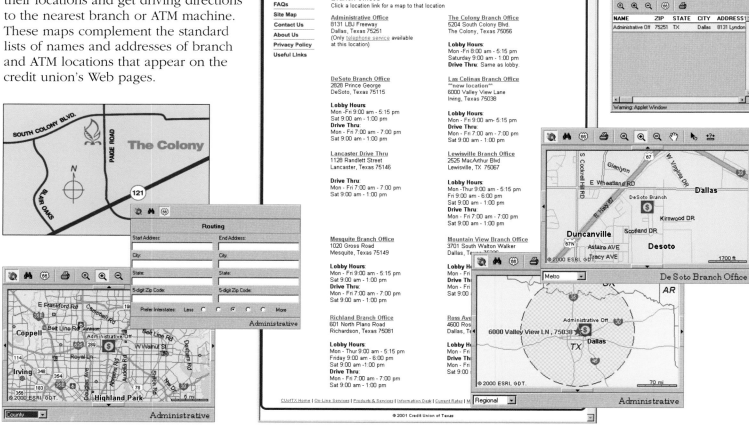

The system

IBM® Enterprise Performance Suite Solution (EZMart), including IBM DB2® Universal Database with Warehouse Manager, IBM xSeries Server, Business Objects (or Simple Attachment Scheme - Online Analytical Processing), EZStore Model from IBM and Modelware International, ESRI ArcView Business Analyst, ESRI *Route*MAP IMS, Unica Corporation Affinium Model (or SAS Enterprise Miner), and IBM Consulting.

The data

Various data from Harland Financial Solutions, Inc., and Axciom Corporation, and data incorporated in ESRI software products.

Acknowledgments

Thanks to Jerry Thompson of the Credit Union of Texas, Kirk Boothe of IBM, and Tony Burns of ESRI.

CREDIT UNION
OF TEXAS

Sharing business information across the Web

5

Chambers of commerce epitomize the concept of networking. In the smallest towns, in the biggest countries, across the largest and most diverse regions of the globe, chambers of commerce and their related associations and organizations help foster effective communication and enterprise. New trade rules and regulations, new ways of doing business, new opportunities—the chambers collect, organize, and share such information among their members to help spur profits and growth.

In one New York City borough, GIS and user-friendly Web pages are dramatically improving the way a local chamber of commerce is shaping the future of effective business networking—plus sharing its information with a public that's worldwide.

GIS in sales and marketing

The Brooklyn Chamber of Commerce is a private, nonprofit business membership association that promotes economic development in the borough and helps local businesses grow. Founded in 1918, its thirteen hundred members make it the largest chamber in New York City and one of the fastest-growing business organizations in the region. Most members are small businesses, but the chamber also represents large manufacturers, wholesale distribution companies, banks, and utilities. Some of its newest members include technology companies moving from nearby Manhattan to Brooklyn to take advantage of more favorable property values.

Sales and marketing are among the chamber's main activities. In the area of advocacy, the chamber also works with other nonprofit entities in promoting Brooklyn's culture, tourism, educational features, civic activities, and general quality of life. In recent years, GIS and the Web have become key tools in advancing the chamber's goals and ambitions.

Brooklyn, with nearly 2.5 million people, is the most populous of New York City's five boroughs.

Building a better organization

As it notes on its Web pages, the Brooklyn Chamber of Commerce hasn't always been the picture of economic health. Chamber officials concede that by the early 1990s, the small business community had little interest in the organization. Some business owners felt that membership wasn't worth the annual fee. Little was happening, some felt, and the chamber had dwindled to representing just a handful of major corporations. By the mid-1990s, new management at the chamber had turned things around and lured back smaller businesses. There were new hires, new ideas, new initiatives, a bigger budget. Membership doubled.

During the past few years, major improvements were made to the chamber's Web presence with the introduction of its new site, iBrooklyn.com. One of the chamber's Web consultants, CommunityCartography, Inc., of Mahwah, New Jersey (a division of HydroQual, Inc., of Mahwah), used ESRI's ArcView GIS and MapObjects® software to help develop interactive maps and information within the site, and chamber officials say that hits on the most popular pages have exceeded expectations.

iBrooklyn.com, introduced in October 2000, provides information about Brooklyn and its business community, culture, people, and neighborhoods.

CommunityCartography, Inc.'s Web site, www.comcarto.com, explains how the company uses GIS for its many clients.

Interactive maps provide views

One of iBrooklyn's primary features is its Business Data Warehouse, a GIS-based collection of interactive maps and information available to anyone who logs on to the Internet. Four major hypertext "views" of Brooklyn are offered: property maps, administrative and political maps, the borough's transportation system, and census data. Zoom-in and zoom-out functions help users pinpoint queries and also see the bigger picture.

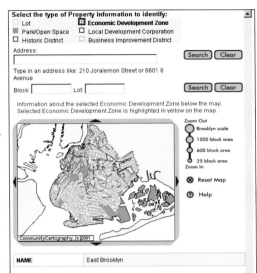

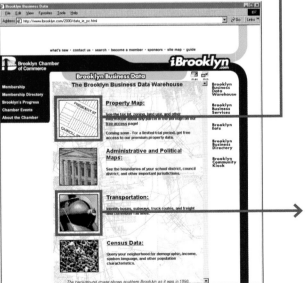

The Property Map feature allows users to locate properties and identify various characteristics, such as whether the plots are near or in an economic development zone or historic district. The owner, building class, zoning, and land use of each property can be found. Here, the East Brooklyn Economic Development Zone is highlighted (in yellow).

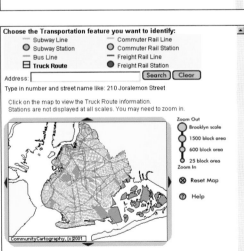

Maps help users identify truck routes and subway, commuter rail, bus, and freight rail lines and stations. Here, truck routes (in red) are displayed across the whole of Brooklyn.

Images on the fly

The various searches launched from the Business Data Warehouse help users find desired information quickly. The maps, like the ones on the previous page, were created by combining many layers of GIS data to form images on the fly. Clicking on a map feature displays the additional data associated with it from its attribute table.

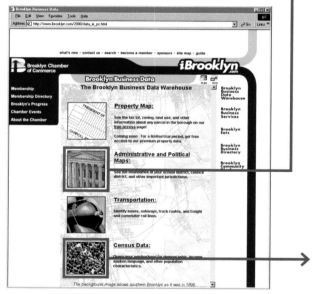

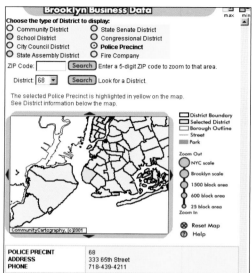

Users of the Web site can access maps showing community, school, city council, state assembly, state senate, and congressional districts, as well as police precincts and fire company areas. Contact information for various representatives is also provided. Here, the 68th Police Precinct is highlighted (in yellow).

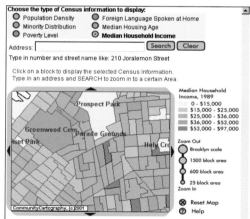

Census data helps identify properties and areas as to density, minority distribution, poverty level, spoken language at home, median household income, and median housing age. This map shows median household income for an area near Prospect Park.

Finding a restaurant

"Brooklyn Eats" is one of iBrooklyn's most popular features. Pick a neighborhood, pick a cuisine, then click if you want to restrict your search to restaurants with parking, smoking, or water views. The data and maps will tell you where to go. More than 250 restaurants and eateries are included in the database. The Web page includes a hyperlinked image of the published *Brooklyn Eats* guidebook, which Internet users can order online. GIS was used to create a map layer of the restaurant data from the guidebook, which is displayed here with other Brooklyn map layers.

Here, a map and seven restaurants are displayed after the user clicks to find Russian cuisine in the Brighton Beach neighborhood. Yellow dots on the map identify the locations, and a listing of restaurants provides additional details.

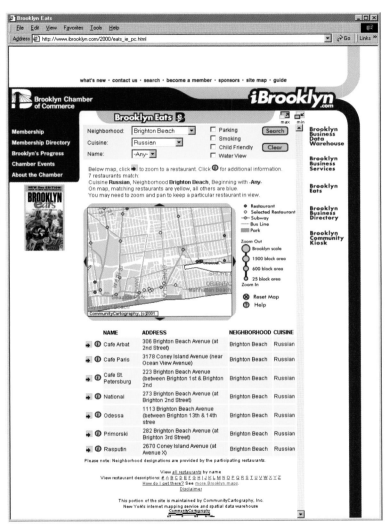

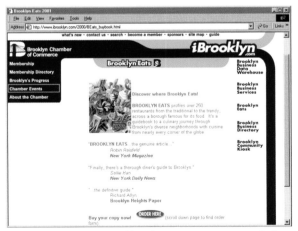

The Web site also enables the Internet user to click and order the printed Brooklyn Eats *book.*

Mining data for solutions

The site's Brooklyn Business Directory allows users to search the chamber of commerce's members database to find all kinds of businesses or other entities in the borough: hotels, banks, clothing stores, supermarkets, manufacturers, technology companies, parks, museums, among many others. Companies and the names of their contact people can be mapped and located by name, and also by category and subcategory. The membership data is updated monthly. There are more than twenty categories of businesses and other entities, ranging alphabetically from "Arts and Entertainment" to "Utilities," with each category having a range of subcategories. For example, the Business Services category alone leads to more than two dozen subcategories ranging from advertising and marketing to check cashing, locksmiths, payroll services, safes and vaults, and waste removal. GIS was a key element in building this functionality.

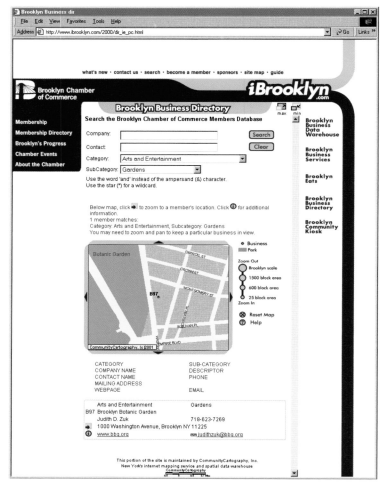

Here, after clicking on Arts and Entertainment and the Gardens subcategory, a listing and map for the Brooklyn Botanical Garden appears, with links to its own Web page and an official contact's e-mail address.

Sizing up a location

Let's say a prospective entrepreneur is interested in a certain parcel at a specific address: 210 Joralemon Street. The iBrooklyn Business Data Warehouse Property map section (below, left) shows where the property is located and what's nearby. In this case, the property is sandwiched between a business improvement district and a historic district. The land is zoned for commercial and manufacturing enterprises. Using the Transportation mapping function (below, right), the prospective buyer can see the site is located along an established truck route, a handy feature for a business that needs to move products and goods.

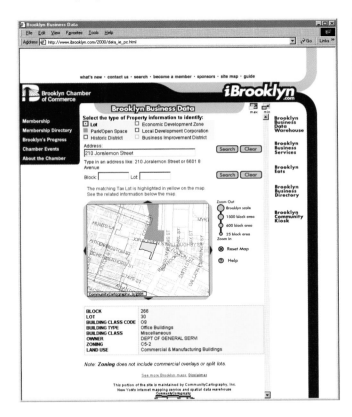

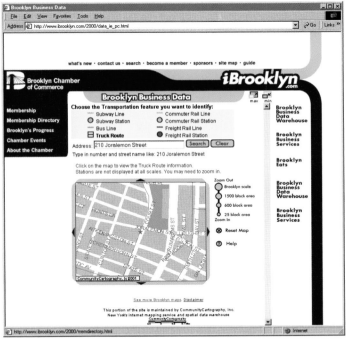

The Transportation mapping function also tells the prospective buyer the site is conveniently near subway and bus routes for workers he might be employing. Using the Brooklyn Eats function, the ever-more-interested property buyer finds numerous restaurants in this Brooklyn Heights area neighborhood. He decides it's a site worthy of further inspection and evaluation. GIS is the vehicle that brought him there.

Plenty of lunching and dining locations are close to the property being evaluated.

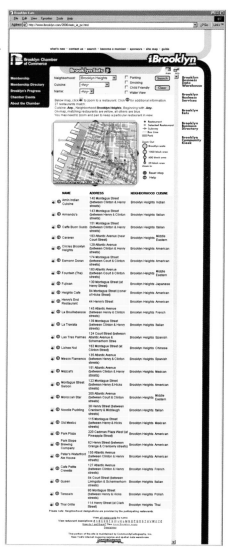

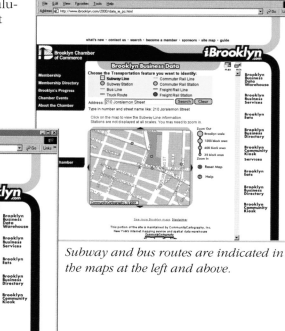

Subway and bus routes are indicated in the maps at the left and above.

The software

Server software: MapObjects IMS 2.0 and MapObjects 2.0; Microsoft Visual Basic® 6.0.

Data development software: ArcView 3.2; Parcel Address Dictionary, a CommunityCartography extension for ArcView.

The data

Various data sources, including Brooklyn Chamber of Commerce (Business Directory and Brooklyn Eats); New York State Department of Transportation (rail lines and truck routes); Empire State Development (economic development zones); New York City Landmarks Preservation Committee (historic districts); U.S. Census (1990 and 2000); Metropolitan Transit Authority New York City Transit (subways and buses); NYC Department of City Planning (tax lot and block basemaps, and administrative districts); NYC Department of Finance (real property assessment information); NYC Department of Business Services (local development corporations); and public databases for parks information.

Acknowledgments

Thanks to Mark Kessler of the Brooklyn Chamber of Commerce, and Ben Miller and Danielle Hartman of CommunityCartography, Inc.

| 0.05 | 0 | 0.05 | 0.1 miles |

6

Mining, collecting, and selling real estate information

The home-building industry is a crowded marketplace with lots of major players—builders, building product manufacturers, land developers, appraisers, real estate investors, investment bankers, and local government officials, among others. In some cases—as between rival builders, for example—the relationships are aggressively competitive, and information is strictly protected. In other cases—as between banks, cities, and builders trying to ink a mutually beneficial business deal—the relationships are characterized by cooperation and the sharing of information. No matter what the situation, the interested parties all need the latest and best information possible on the real estate industry.

One of America's premier sources of such information is providing an award-winning GIS application covering scores of U.S. housing markets. The appeal and value of the product is fundamental: Time is money, and anything that saves time can potentially boost the bottom line in profits.

Establishing a presence

The Meyers Group, with corporate headquarters in Irvine, California, is a supplier of market information, analysis, and consulting services to the residential development industry, using Internet-based technologies and proprietary software. Founded in Del Mar, California, in 1985, it's now the nation's top provider of new-home real estate information, covering two million new homes and the top seventy-five U.S. housing markets. The company is a "knowledge partner" to more than three thousand organizations, helping clients through effective use of market intelligence and competitive information.

The Meyers Group, on the Web at www.meyersgroup.com, has numerous offices and housing market footholds throughout the United States.

Range of products

Among The Meyers Group's principal products are Residential Pro GIS 2000, a tool for analyzing the new housing market; Land Pro, a tool for tracking proposed new home development; and the Homebuilder Database, an extensive listing of contact information for the housing industry. All three are available on a subscription basis on CD–ROM. The Meyers Group also has a business-to-business Web site allowing customers to purchase market information and analysis online. Eventually the company plans to offer all of its products online.

In particular, Residential Pro is a good example of how homebuilders and other real estate consultants can employ the analytical tools of GIS to find, sort, and more effectively use the data flowing in from new home research. Residential Pro, which uses ESRI's MapObjects software, is the first housing market report on CD–ROM. It's a user-friendly software application that saves time and money when it comes to analyzing the new housing market and developing both customized and standardized reports. It provides instant, up-to-date, color maps of housing projects, as well as other visual information such as detailed floor plans and elevations, monthly sales rates, buyer profiles, and product descriptions.

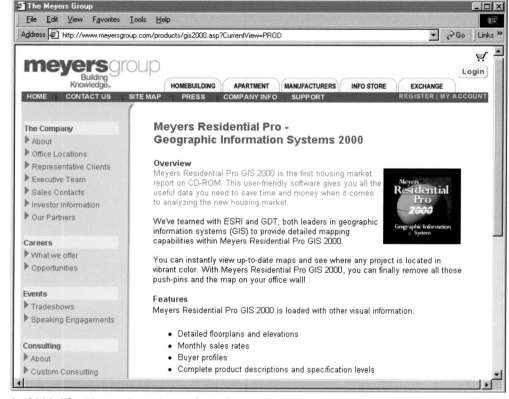

In 2000, The Meyers Group's Residential Pro CD–ROM received first place in ESRI's MapObjects Application Contest, which judged applications on functionality, documentation, problem-solving, and technical elegance.

Searching with GIS

There are a number of ways for users of Residential Pro to zero in on housing markets for study and analysis. One way is using basic GIS map tools to isolate specific geographic areas. In the examples on this page, drawing a rectangle around housing markets in the Oregon and Washington area is a way to focus on projects in that region. Drawing a circle around markets in Central California is the beginning of an inquiry for that area. And deftly casting a polygon around the Southern California region sets up that part of the state for further exploration.

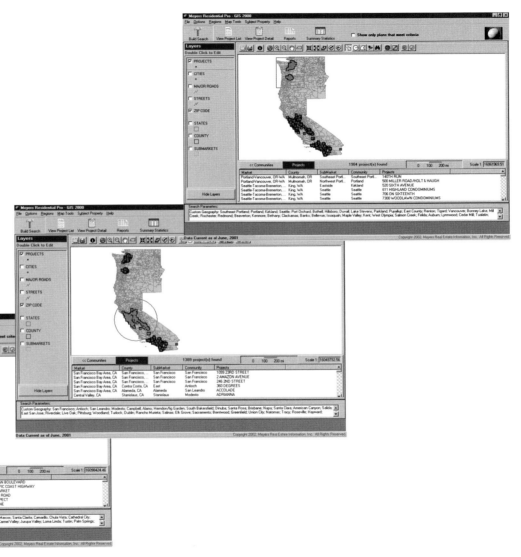

One user's benefits

Ryland Homes, which started in 1967 and is based in Calabasas, California, has become one of the largest home builders in the United States, with more than 180,000 houses constructed. Ryland uses Residential Pro to study sales and pricing trends in housing markets where the firm currently builds homes, as well as markets they are interested in. In the past, obtaining the latest and best market information meant digging for long hours to find the material, then more time invested in writing reports and sticking pushpins into a map on the office wall. In real estate, as in so many other endeavors involving research, sales, and marketing, computers and GIS are changing the dynamics of how information is gathered and decisions are made. Residential Pro gives firms like Ryland detailed maps and information on housing "hot spots" throughout the country—an example of which is San Diego County, California.

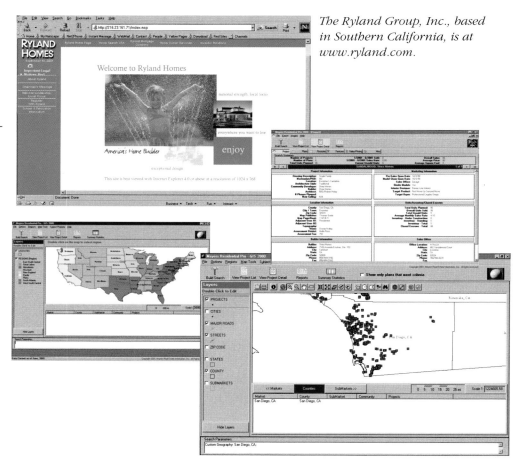

The Ryland Group, Inc., based in Southern California, is at www.ryland.com.

Residential Pro uses ESRI's MapObjects *software to map and illustrate housing markets throughout the United States. Major regions can be selected, such as the western coastal region of California, Oregon, and Washington. The so-named Pacific region can be examined, then narrowed to the San Diego County, California, market. The user can pinpoint even more precisely and take a detailed look at the "Coastal North" submarket of San Diego. The map at the bottom shows various housing projects by different builders.*

Summary stats

Residential Pro enables Ryland and other users to quickly call up summary statistics reports organized by housing market. Here, simply clicking on a name such as "San Diego, CA" instantly produces a detailed report for a six-month time period, showing sales, canceled sales, and rates of sales; median prices and size of homes by square footage; and average prices and square footage. The map below shows how projects, cities, and major roads are mapped for a wide area of southern San Diego County.

Residential Pro provides quick navigation from a particular county and housing market to a full statistical report that's already typed, formatted, and ready for printing.

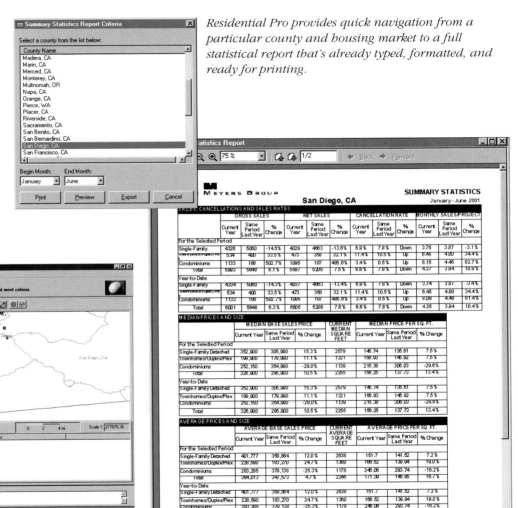

Building queries

Residential Pro also has various attribute filters with which users can build queries. In this case, asking to see single-family homes with lot sizes from 7,500 square feet to 8,999 square feet produces a map with red dots showing those types of homes in the Coastal North submarket, plus a table below the map that displays housing projects further identified by community and project name.

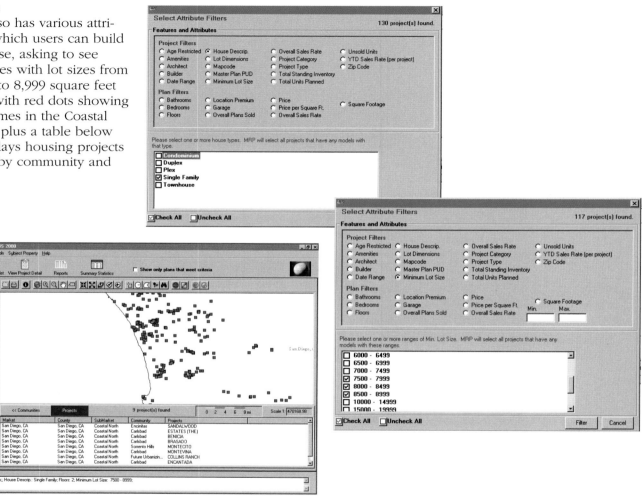

Once a user has identified a range of projects meeting certain criteria, it's possible to focus on one or more of the projects with a mouse click and perform additional analysis.

Zeroing in on a project

From the list of projects mapped on the previous page, a user can highlight a specific development and view more detailed information about that project. Residential Pro can quickly generate a report that provides location, marketing, and builder information for a given project, in addition to specifics on the number of units, inventory, and closed escrows, plus a helpful guide to sales office and contact information. Residential Pro also produces tables that provide details about specific layouts of homes within a project, such as pricing; pricing per square foot; lot and exterior features; appliances and interior features; bathroom and flooring features; financing information; and names of local schools.

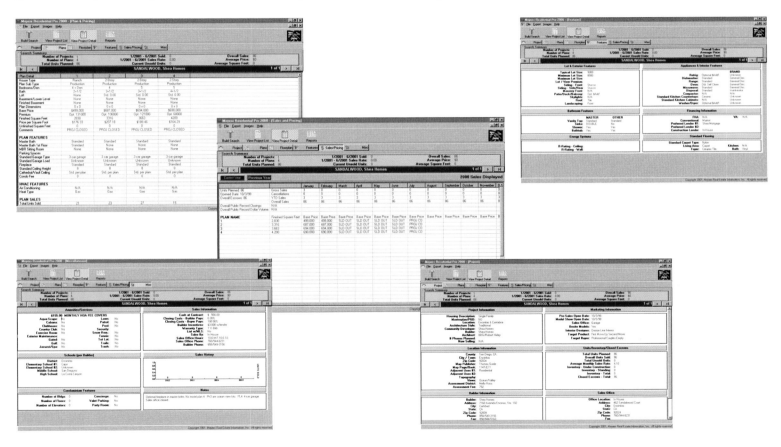

Photos, drawings, details

Residential Pro also lets the user see even more detailed information on floor plans, including a photo of the model and floor plan drawing, as well as facts about sales, fees, schools, and other features. This type of information has been available in the past in the form of brochures and other materials that require extensive use of employee time to produce. Residential Pro, relying on the steadily increasing speeds and capacities of computers, GIS mapping, and data analysis, turns what could be hours of labor into literally seconds of work.

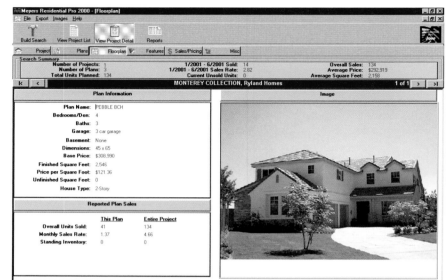

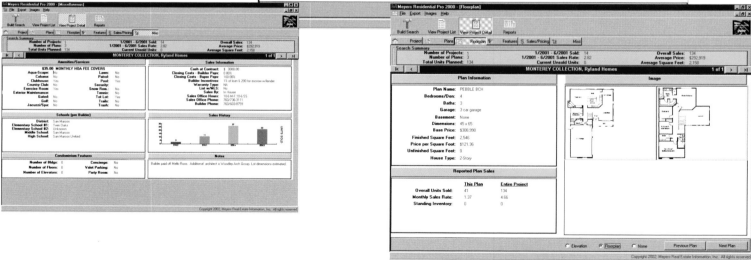

The software

Microsoft Access and Microsoft Visual Basic; ActiveReports, Data Dynamics, Ltd.; ESRI MapObjects.

CD–ROM system requirements

100-MHz PC or higher recommended; 32 MB of RAM recommended; VGA or higher resolution monitor; screen resolution 800 × 600 or higher; minimum 300 MB or more of free hard-disk space; CD–ROM drive; Microsoft Windows 95, Windows 98, or Windows NT version 4.0 SP5, with ODBC version 3.5 or greater; a mouse or other pointing device supported by Windows.

The data

The Meyers Group project data and GDT Dynamap/2000 data.

Acknowledgments

Thanks to Hunter Robbins and Tony Dulkis of The Meyers Group, Inc., Leslie Sinfield of Ryland Homes, and Colleen Schelde of ESRI.

7

Growing a business base through "economic gardening"

For a number of progressive cities, the new wave in economic development centers on cultivating, strengthening, and nurturing existing businesses rather than the gamble of attracting new enterprise. Methods include helping local businesses recruit and train employees, assisting firms in obtaining capital funding, cooperating with companies to develop planning and marketing strategies, fostering media contacts, and providing data analysis, among other endeavors. "Economic gardening" is the term for the trend, and the idea is growing.

Southern California's Inland Empire region encompasses parts of Riverside, San Bernardino, and Los Angeles counties. It's a hotbed of growth and economic development, and one city's experience with economic gardening shows how GIS can play a major part in the movement.

A city helping businesses

Lake Elsinore is a city of thirty thousand lying alongside Interstate 15 in western Riverside County, about an hour and a half's drive from downtown Los Angeles. Because of its location and semirural nature, the city struggled for many years to capture quality business and commercial development that often ended up locating in points north and south. In recent decades, increasing commercial, retail, and residential development along the north–south I-15 freeway corridor began to change that, and by the late 1990s the city was one of a small handful in the region to take a proactive role with economic gardening.

Working with California State University, San Bernardino, whose Community–University Partnerships program provided funding, Lake Elsinore in summer 2000 commenced an ongoing pilot program that is helping local businesses. GIS mapping and data analysis figure importantly in the effort.

Geographically, Lake Elsinore lies between Los Angeles and San Diego, in Southern California. On the Web, the city is at www.lake-elsinore.org.

Helping a retailer

California Skier is a boat sales and service firm in Lake Elsinore, specializing in MasterCraft vessels, which are high-end, tournament ski boats. Formerly based in Riverside (a larger city to the northeast), California Skier moved to Lake Elsinore in 1997 primarily because the city's well-known lake and namesake provided a perfect natural feature for helping to showcase and demonstrate the boats and equipment it sells. The company also offers boat-driving clinics and water-skiing and wakeboarding lessons on the lake, which, at about 3,000 acres, is Southern California's largest natural lake.

As the economic gardening project began moving forward, company and city staff met and identified a number of business goals to pursue. They wanted to know how California Skier's market share compared to competitors, as well as how the firm could improve its market share and sales, increase its service-related business, and better target future advertising and promotion efforts.

California Skier's Web site, www.californiaskier.com, shows why it's a major retailer for boat buyers in Southern California. Its location near the Lake Elsinore Aquatic Park is just one example of how geography can be important to a company's marketing and sales efforts.

Customer profiling

To help California Skier, Lake Elsinore's GIS team used ArcView Business Analyst to find new customers based on profiles of current customers. The team first collected existing customer information from California Skier's database in electronic format. The data provided complete address information, but did not have a spatial aspect that allowed it to be mapped easily. Using Business Analyst, the team geocoded the customers and created a spatial data layer that was overlaid with a census block group layer. The team could then demographically profile the selected block group areas where the existing customers lived to help California Skier know more about the types of people—marital status, home ownership status, income, and other variables—who buy high-end ski boats. The GIS analysis identified similar census block group areas where targeted advertising could be aimed.

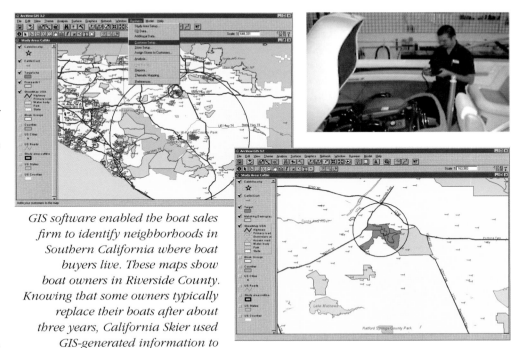

GIS software enabled the boat sales firm to identify neighborhoods in Southern California where boat buyers live. These maps show boat owners in Riverside County. Knowing that some owners typically replace their boats after about three years, California Skier used GIS-generated information to target advertising to owners who might be ready to buy a new boat, as well as those who might need their present boats serviced.

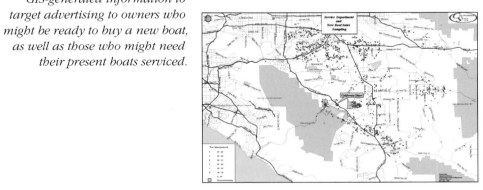

Informing customers

California Skier's owner, Chuck Sacks, knew that some of his prospective customers didn't realize how close the business was to them. After the firm's move from Riverside south to Lake Elsinore, some folks thought the company was now farther away from major population centers than it really was. Because California Skier attends and displays boats and wares at four major boat shows in Southern California each year, the firm needed a more effective way of communicating just how conveniently located it is.

That's where ArcView Business Analyst came in handy again. The city's GIS team used the software to make large-size display maps and also smaller handout maps showing the mileage and driving times from each of the major boat shows to the doorstep of California Skier. The software takes route information and overlays it with basemap data to create professional, customized images; it also calculates the driving times.

For throngs of people at crowded regional shows, visually displaying the exact location of the company in comparison to the whole of Southern California proved to be an effective marketing move. Telling customers where your business is and how to get there is one thing; showing them is better.

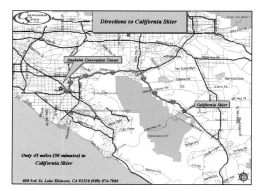

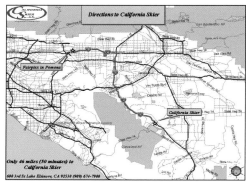

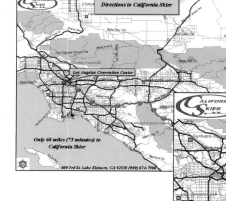

These GIS-generated map images, enlarged and reproduced on large displays at boat shows, gave California Skier an enhanced degree of professionalism, along with something eye-catching that other vendors didn't have.

Planning for the future

California Skier specializes in one major line of high-end, tournament ski boats, but it has an eye on expanding its sales in the future by offering vessels for the more average boating enthusiast. Lake Elsinore's GIS team used ArcView Business Analyst to geocode the locations of all boat owners in five Southern California counties, along with the make of boats. The team also produced charts that, along with maps, provided a clear visual image of the boat-buying marketplace. California Skier was able to see which lines of boats were most popular in different subregions, and the new, customized information gave the company insights on how it might focus sales, marketing, and promotion in the future.

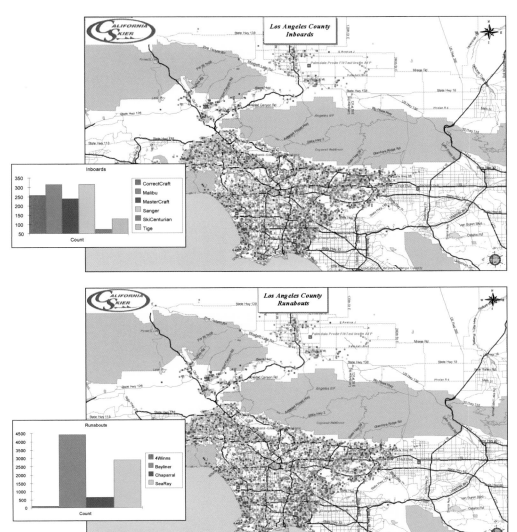

Working with a specialty niche firm

Totally Themed, Inc., is one of Lake Elsinore's most unique businesses. The company specializes in custom design and fabrication services for themed environments. Owned by Steve and Vicky Wallace, the company provides a variety of services for major theme parks, hotels, casinos, restaurants, and retail establishments.

Being creative, the firm was looking for new ways to market itself and spread the word about its products and services. The city's economic gardening program helped in various ways, and GIS played a role.

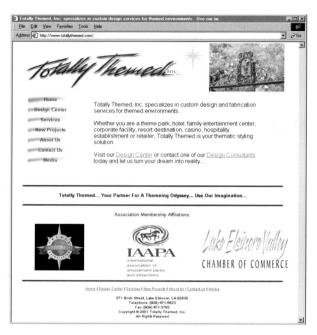

Totally Themed's Web site, www.totallythemed.com, provides a glimpse of the specialized and unique fabrication work the company does for amusement parks and other enterprises.

Tapping the labor force

Because of the nature of its work, Totally Themed has very specialized needs in the areas of welding, carpentry, fiberglass, and metal fabrication. It uses mostly local businesses to supply those services; it also hires and contracts with skilled laborers from the immediate region and beyond.

Using iMarket® data and ArcView Business Analyst, the GIS team was able to help the company locate the closest available subcontractors, depending on the location of the job. Maps show the locations, and the iMarket reports give Totally Themed information about the individual companies.

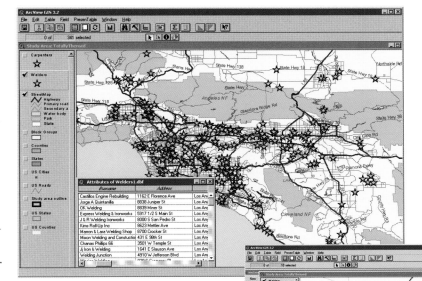

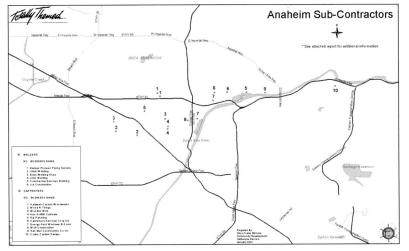

Maps like these gave Totally Themed a view of where it could find welders and carpenters. The maps also helped in planning and setting up various jobs, as well as reducing costs.

Mapping a national customer base

Totally Themed's relationships with amusement parks are central to its business success; the company has worked with some of the biggest and best. But even the company's owners weren't fully aware of just how many amusement parks there were across the United States. As part of its effort to help the company, the city's GIS team used iMarket data and ArcView Business Analyst to plot the locations of scores of amusement parks on a map, which gave company owners an enhanced view and sense of this major segment of their market.

The maps, along with other data-rich written materials the city was able to provide as part of the economic gardening effort, gave Totally Themed a great new marketing idea. The company held a major open house where examples of its work were showcased to prospective clients who came as invited guests. As a result of that very successful show and presentation, Totally Themed immediately signed up a number of new clients who needed and wanted the firm's unique skills and abilities.

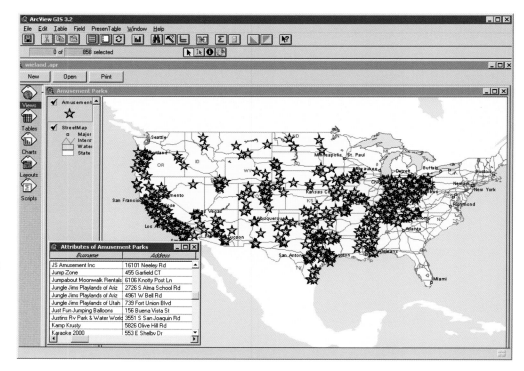

GIS business data and mapping functions produced a locator map that proved valuable in the company's overall marketing and sales effort.

Assisting a construction contractor

GBC Concrete & Masonry Construction, Inc., of Lake Elsinore, is a subcontractor specializing in mid- to large-size commercial jobs ranging from about a half-million dollars to $2 million. The company, which employs about 180 people, performs concrete and masonry work in both the public and private sectors. Projects include auto dealerships, major retail chain stores, and self-storage firms throughout Southern California. The company also does work in Nevada, Arizona, and Oregon.

The company owner, Tom Daniel, had a solid grasp of who his existing customers were and where he was laying brick, mortar, and cement. His business was doing well and he knew there were other projects he could get his hands on, but he didn't have the time to do a lot of research. Economic gardening and GIS provided an opportunity for the company to learn more about itself, more about recent trends in the construction industry in general, and what the future might hold for each.

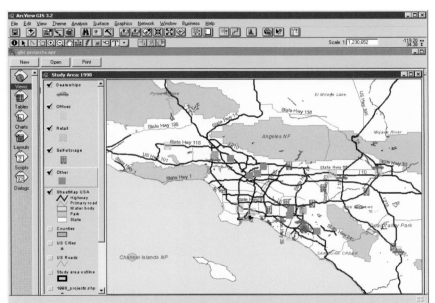

GIS-generated maps like this one gave GBC a clearer picture that many of its jobs were alongside heavily traveled freeways. Realizing this, the company started placing advertising banners at its work sites more extensively than it had in the past. It was the visual power of the map that generated a bright idea about how to increase the company's profile and in turn attract more business and profits.

A quick glimpse of GBC's history
GBC wanted to know how its business had progressed or changed over a four-year period. Using spreadsheet data in electronic format and ArcView Business Analyst, the city's GIS team made maps and charts showing how the company's projects had changed over the period in terms of type, scope, and size. Knowing what types of jobs were on the increase or decrease over time helped the company make better business decisions. For example, GBC realized that auto dealerships and self-storage facilities accounted for a major chunk of its business. To make sure the firm would not become too dependent on those types of construction work, the company owner took steps to identify other types of jobs he wanted to bid on and win, such as country club buildings and schools, among others. Using GIS and maps, the company was able to shift its position and tap an ever-widening market for construction jobs.

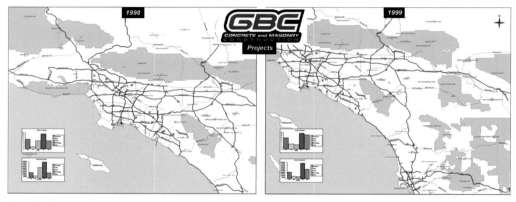

Maps and charts gave GBC an impressive visual picture of the firm's place in a changing marketplace over a four-year period. It also helped in making smart business decisions about where and when to expand into different markets.

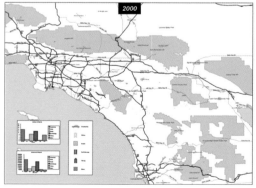
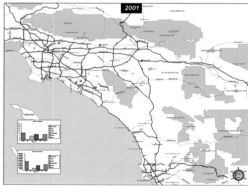

The company's Web address is www.gbcconstruction.com.

A look at the market

GBC wanted to see where new construction "hot spots" were in Southern California, its primary area of operations. The GIS team developed a database from the *Southern California Construction Bulletin,* a weekly publication that details construction work throughout the region. Information on various projects, including the type of job and its location, was then mapped so the company could see the scope of building activity. Knowing this information helped GBC learn about, bid for, and win jobs it would otherwise have missed.

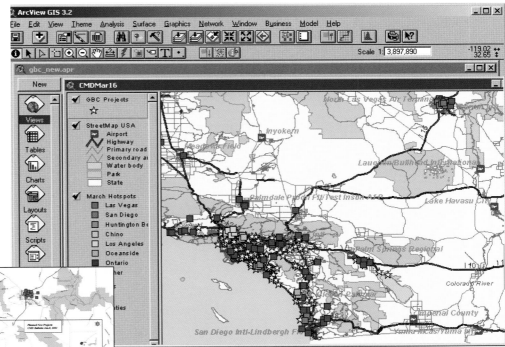

Professional-looking maps also gave the company a leg up on the competition. Bids are often won after formal business presentations made with people sitting around a conference table. GIS-related maps and charts produced by Lake Elsinore's economic gardening team helped GBC make stronger and more effective presentations in its quests to win business. The colored squares indicate new construction "hot spots" in different parts of the greater Southern California region and Las Vegas area. Stars represent locations of GBC's projects.

The software

ArcView GIS, ArcView Business Analyst, Network Analyst, and StreetMap™ extensions, MarketPlace by iMarket Inc., and Microsoft Access.

The data

StreetMap and MarketPlace iMarket data; new construction data from the *Southern California Construction Bulletin* (Construction Market Data Group); and private data from the companies featured.

Acknowledgments

Thanks to Marlene Best, Catheryne W. Barrozo, and Richard A. Hess of the City of Lake Elsinore; Chuck Sacks of California Skier; Steve and Vicky Wallace of Totally Themed, Inc.; and Tom Daniel of GBC Concrete & Masonry Construction, Inc. Thanks also to Lee Hanson and the Community–University Partnerships program at California State University, San Bernardino.

8

Economic development and GIS

There is more than one way to expand the business base within a city. Economic gardening is proving a fertile concept in many locales. Other cities, meanwhile, are using interactive Web pages to feature their retail, commercial, and industrial prowess. Like well-crafted resumes, customized Web sites are powerful expressions of what a city can provide in the way of business-related opportunities to entrepreneurs, current residents, prospective citizens, travelers, shoppers, and commuters who pass through the city during their daily drives to and from work.

One Southern California city is discovering the benefits of helping its business community with an award-winning Web site that uses GIS in a major way. Retail vacancy rates at local shopping centers have dropped significantly, more retail and business centers are being built, and there's a new global awareness of the business opportunities and advantages in this fast-growing city.

Telling its own story

Rancho Cucamonga, with a population of about 132,700, lies near the interstate 10 and 15 freeway corridors that intersect near San Bernardino, California. Like much of Southern California, the city's agriculture and open space have been giving way in recent years to residential, retail, commercial, office, and industrial development. The story of this regional growth has been told for decades in many forums, including newspapers and magazines. Today, Rancho Cucamonga's Redevelopment Agency is using GIS mapping technology to provide its own "show and tell" on the Internet. Whether it's helping to market the city itself or providing tools for the local, national, and worldwide business communities, the new technology paints a picture that's as visually dramatic as it is informative.

Rancho Cucamonga is due east of Los Angeles and is part of Southern California's fast-growing Inland Empire region.

Beyond the brochure

Printed brochures, binders full of data, and glossy handout photos are one way to tell a story, and for years cities have used them to attract new people and businesses. For Rancho Cucamonga, the city's popular "INside Rancho" Web site is the modern mode of this type of promotion. INside Rancho—rich with digital and aerial photos, tables, interactive maps, query functions, and other features—was developed in part by GIS Planning, of Berkeley, California, using ESRI's MapObjects software. The site's main page contains quick links to a wealth of additional information: city facts, local and regional demographics, government contacts, and, for the business community in particular, instant and easily navigable Web connections to retail, office, and industrial site information.

GIS Planning's Web site, www.gisplanning.com, tells Internet users about the cities and other clients that have benefited from GIS software and systems.

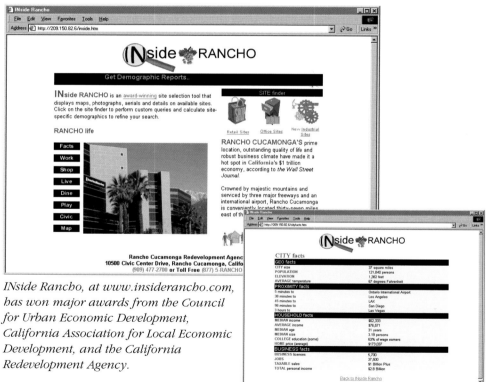

INside Rancho, at www.insiderancho.com, has won major awards from the Council for Urban Economic Development, California Association for Local Economic Development, and the California Redevelopment Agency.

Mining retail site information

The retail site locator helps the business community as well as the general public research commercial real estate in Rancho Cucamonga. Existing retail sites, along with parcels available for development, can be identified or found by name, square footage, and general location, and then viewed in greater detail.

In this example, the Retail Sites locator tells the user about an existing retail center in the west side of the city and what it has to offer in the way of traffic counts, acreage, major tenants, and other key business information.

A link at the bottom of the Retail Sites locator page leads to a detailed demographics summary for the area.

Besides online access to detailed property information, a special feature allows real estate brokers and city staff to update property and lease space information online. This updated information is immediately displayed on the page.

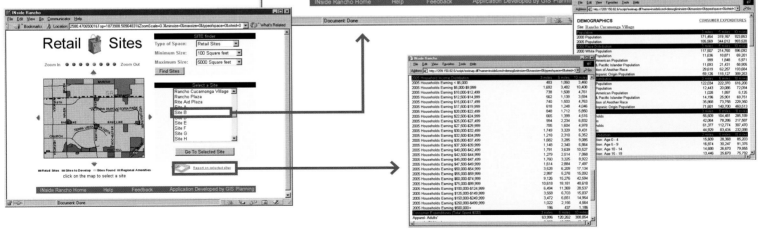

In this case, the site locator displays property in the eastern part of Rancho Cucamonga that is ripe for retail development. An aerial view of the property is provided, and, like the example on the previous page, there's a link to a real estate broker. The demographic data, provided by another link, includes information about people who live near the area, with breakdowns by age, race, type of household, income, and consumer expenditures.

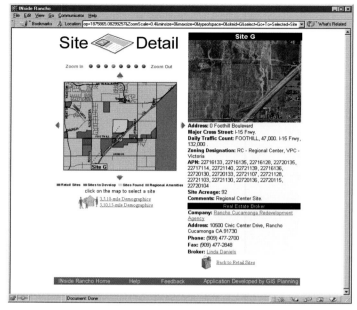

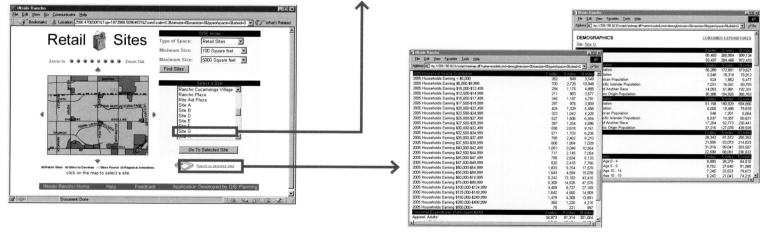

Checking out industrial zones

An easy navigation to the Industrial Zones page lets viewers see a color-coded map of these zones in the city, and the properties can be individually selected by category, such as buildings for sale, space for lease, or bare land. A user can also simply click on a property to learn more about it, or use square footage as a means of finding a suitable plot. The Web pages use aerial photography to help tell the story, and rail and truck routes are also indicated on the maps.

City officials say the GIS technology has radically reduced the time it takes to research and prepare reports when information is requested about specific land parcels. In the past, such reports could take hours to complete. With GIS, the reports can be generated in a few minutes with the click of a mouse.

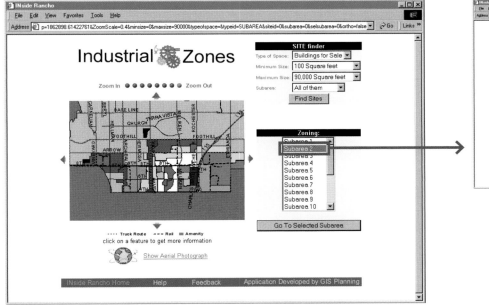

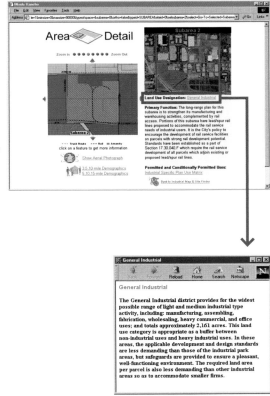

Merely clicking on the red parcel or clicking by its name quickly identifies it as prime land for manufacturing and warehousing facilities, with plans by the city to also provide rail access. Additional navigation informs the user more about land-use designations and what they mean.

For the Industrial Zones pages, the heart of INside Rancho is the zoomable, interactive mapping function, coupled with the aerial photographs and links to zoning and property-use information. These examples further show how maps can be manipulated with just a few mouse clicks, and how photos help to explain what specific properties look like from the air. In spring 2002, developers of INside Rancho were in the process of expanding the Web site to include searches for office space to complement the retail and industrial site searching capabilities.

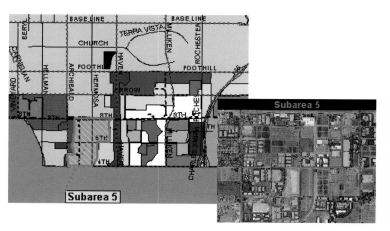

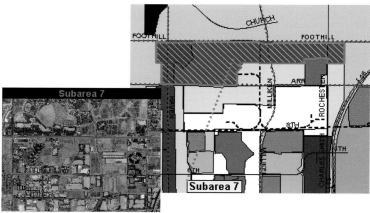

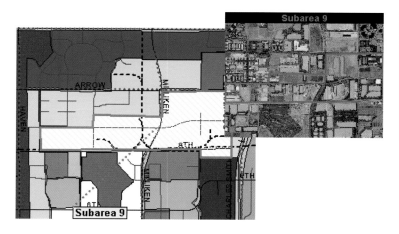

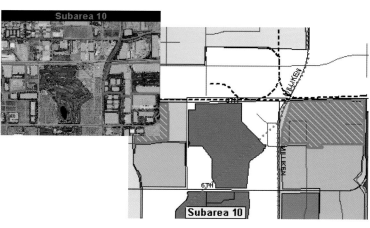

A guide to the region

INside Rancho also serves as a guide to other features in the city and immediate region, many of which are vital to the business community. The site finder page is the starting point for an Internet visit to the local chamber of commerce, where a variety of business-related information is available; Ontario International Airport, a major transportation hub for business travelers; Metrolink, an important Southern California rail system that helps link the Inland Empire to major cities such as Los Angeles and San Diego; and Burlington Northern Santa Fe railroad, one of North America's primary freight haulers. The site finder also links to other sites with information on golf, recreation, and city government, as well as major employers in the area and the nature of the local labor force.

A few clicks on the site and a businessperson knows how and where to fly in and out of the area; where to stay; where to catch the commuter train; how to ship freight; where to take a client to lunch; where to relax or do business over a round of golf; and how and where to find city officials to discuss the big project that's planned or under way.

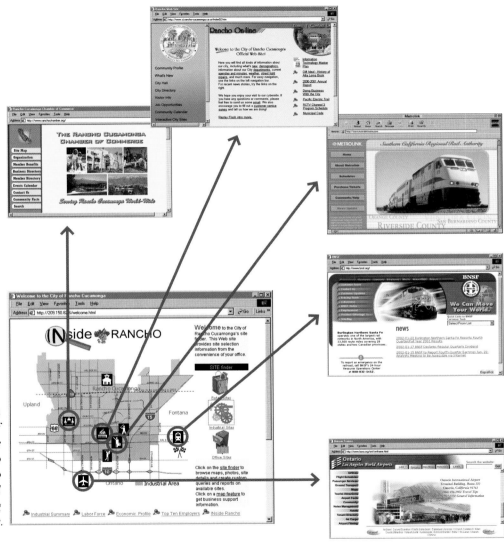

The system

Client side: Browser type and version supported: Netscape® 3.x and Microsoft Internet Explorer 3.02 or higher (JavaScript™ must be enabled).

Client application: HTML and JavaScript.

Web server: HPLC3 NetServer, Windows NT Advanced Server 4.0., 450 MHz dual processor, 512 MB RAM.

Firewall/Proxy software: IBM AIX® firewall.

Map server: Windows NT, 450 MHz dual processor, 512 MB RAM.

Development environment: Microsoft Visual Basic 6, MapObjects software from ESRI.

The data

Microsoft Access databases, aerial photography, and photos of properties.

Acknowledgments

Thanks to William Alexander, Linda Daniels, and Flavio H. Nuñez of the City of Rancho Cucamonga; Pablo Monzon and Anatalio Ubalde of GIS Planning; Nancy Sappington of ESRI; and Cathy Wahlstrom, formerly with the City of Rancho Cucamonga and currently with the City of Ontario. Thanks also to Norm MacKenzie of the Rancho Cucamonga Chamber of Commerce; Maria Tesoro of Ontario International Airport; Eliza Shamshian of Metrolink; and Pat Hiatte of Burlington Northern Santa Fe.

9

Streamlining lawn care and exploring marketing areas

For many homeowners, nothing beats a lush lawn. Unfortunately, not everybody has a thumb that's green enough to make it happen consistently. That's where the lawn care professional steps in: the local expert—sometimes a small businessperson—who knows how and when to fertilize, what products to use, how often to mow, and the best strategies for dealing with insects and weeds.

For a long time, a solid work ethic and the right tools and products were enough to make a lawn care business successful. For many gardening entrepreneurs, those ingredients still work. But today, computers and GIS software are becoming part of the business of caring for grass, and one lawn care professional in Ontario, Canada, is showing how it's done.

Building a business

Dr. Green Lawncare is one of the fastest-growing lawn care firms in southwestern Ontario. The company, founded by Lou Van Haastrecht in 1988, is a classic example of a small business quickly getting bigger. Lou's wife, Lorraine, joined the firm in 1992, and each of their six children has an active role in the family business. Starting with about fifteen hundred customers in the late 1980s and early 1990s, the company now has about fourteen thousand customers and employs forty to fifty workers from spring to late fall.

Dr. Green Lawncare belongs to a number of professional organizations, including Landscape Ontario, and is an international member of the Professional Lawn Care Association of America.

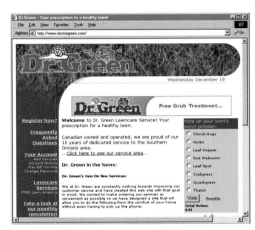

Dr. Green Lawncare's Web site, at www.doctorgreen.com, provides information on a range of services and also offers free tips on maintaining a healthy lawn.

Providing a service

Dr. Green Lawncare has a fleet of about twenty trucks, each driven by a lawn care specialist on a specific route. Each day, those specialists combined provide fertilizing, weed control, and other services to eight hundred to nine hundred customers. Each service call takes about ten to fifteen minutes. Dealing with 75,000 customers each season, and getting vehicles and specialists to the right locations as quickly as possible, is a tough task. At one point, company managers were concerned that the specialists were losing too much valuable time just trying to find customer locations. The use of standard maps just wasn't getting the job done.

Knowing that change was necessary, the company looked for help. DMTI Spatial, Inc., a leading North American GIS consulting firm, recommended the company use its CanMap RouteLogistics, a data application developed with ESRI's ArcLogistics Route. It is a product that helps fleet owners reduce operating costs, improve routing and scheduling, and realize improved customer relations through better on-time delivery of services.

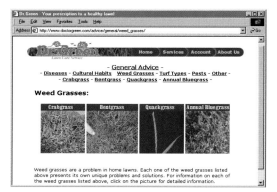

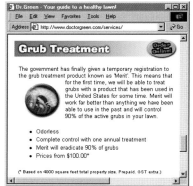

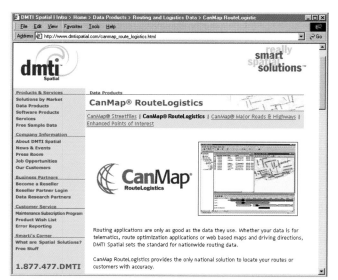

DMTI Spatial, Inc., on the Web at www.dmtispatial.com and www.desktopmapping.com, is a major Canadian GIS product and solutions provider that helped Dr. Green Lawncare streamline its fleet operations. DMTI Spatial has its headquarters in Markham, Ontario.

Dr. Green Lawncare's service area is in a part of southwestern Ontario known as the Golden Horseshoe. It's an area that includes several communities of various sizes throughout the greater Toronto area. Streamlining and GIS-based management of the company's routes started with loading key information into a computer and organizing it: names and addresses of lawn care clients, vehicle start and stop times, the number of minutes that lawn care specialists will be at given locations, types of service each customer will receive, among other factors.

Dr. Green offers a range of service levels ranging from very basic to very complete, and the ability of the GIS software to keep it all straight and display it spatially helps managers see trends, spot problems, improve service, and reduce transportation costs.

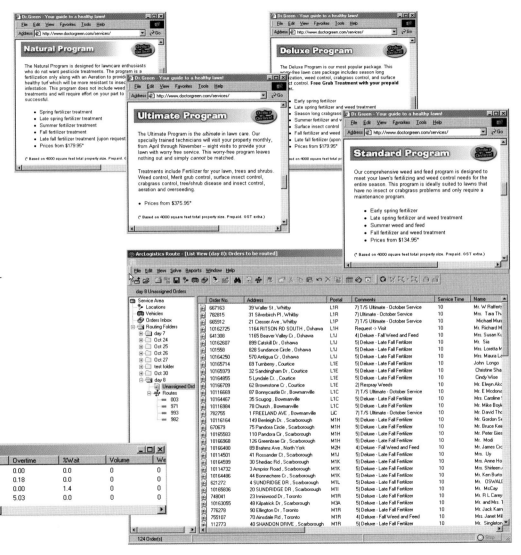

Visualizing routes

With the software up and running, dispatchers and managers can better see where service technicians will be on any given day. Maps like the ones on these pages use different colors to show, for example, which service techs will be working in which sectors of Dr. Green's territory. One map shows routes over a wide area, while the other map displays the routes zoomed in, with numbered service stops more clearly discernible as specific locations.

ArcLogistics Route can also instantly produce graphic images that help businesses more clearly see what a service tech's or driver's workday actually looks like against a time scale, as the illustration on this page shows. For example, the tech on Route 003 has a number of short-term service calls that are geographically close together through the morning hours. The worker takes a lunch break at 11 A.M., then has fewer service calls in the early-through-mid-afternoon, with longer drive times in between.

The tech on Route 971 has a stop at 3 P.M., then a cluster of calls after 4 P.M., while the tech on Route 993 has some long service calls from about 7:30 A.M. to just after 8. The tech on Route 982 is lucky or unlucky, as the case may be: he's working for only half the day.

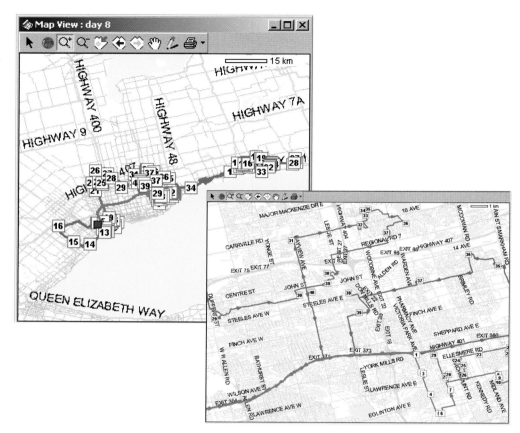

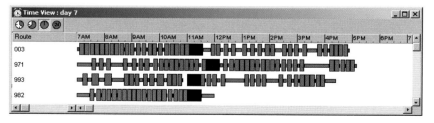

Maps, directions, reports

In many companies, service techs and drivers have to juggle wide-format spreadsheets and route reports in one hand, then open separate map books with the other hand as eyes flash back and forth, trying to make sense of where the next route stop or service call is supposed to be.

That doesn't happen with GIS-based routing systems like the ones used by Dr. Green. On a daily basis, ArcLogistics Route—either by itself or coupled with other software products like the ones developed by DMTI and others—can produce route maps and directions in one handy format. The maps on this page display Route 003 in two views: one shows a cluster of stops near the lakeside, and fewer and more widely dispersed stops farther inland; the other map comes with printed, step-by-step, stop-by-stop directions for getting from one service call to the next.

Dispatchers can also produce their own summaries that are calculated and tabulated by the computer working with its software. These summaries help managers and business owners make informed decisions about routing and help show them how changes in routing can enhance their bottom line.

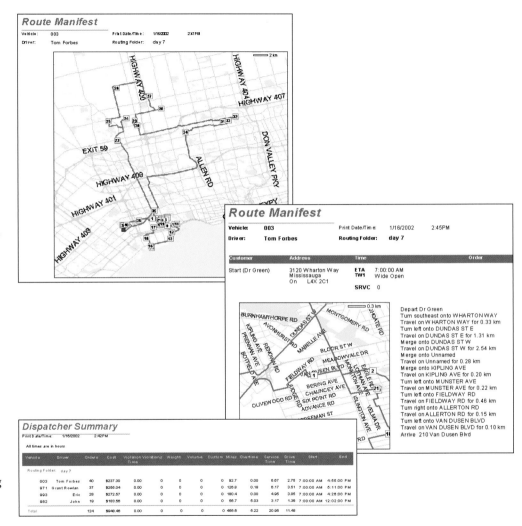

GIS for market analysis

Dr. Green uses GIS for more than just route management. ESRI's ArcView 8.1 and ArcMap software help the company learn about and analyze the market for lawn care services throughout its region. After geocoding the company's existing customers (as illustrated by the map below left that shows dark-colored dots), additional maps showing specific target market areas are generated. The map in the middle shows a primary target market area identified with red dots, a secondary target market area with green dots, and a tertiary target market area with blue dots.

Using the GIS software and related marketing information products and data provided by DMTI Spatial, Dr. Green discovered that the primary target market area, a compact geographic region in and around the Toronto suburb of Mississauga, had a potential to generate as much as $8.9 million in gross sales. The secondary target market area, a subregion north of Toronto that includes Richmond Hill and Markham, had a potential of nearly $7.5 million in gross sales. And the third target market area, which includes a number of widely spread suburbs farther out from Toronto, had a potential of $6.5 million in gross sales.

The map below right, which includes a layer of roads laid down under the target market areas, is the starting point for further examination of the transportation system Dr. Green would encounter should the company decide to expand into a particular neighborhood or part of a targeted market area.

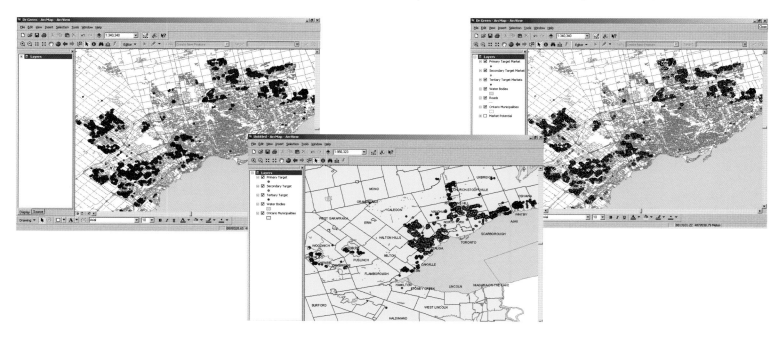

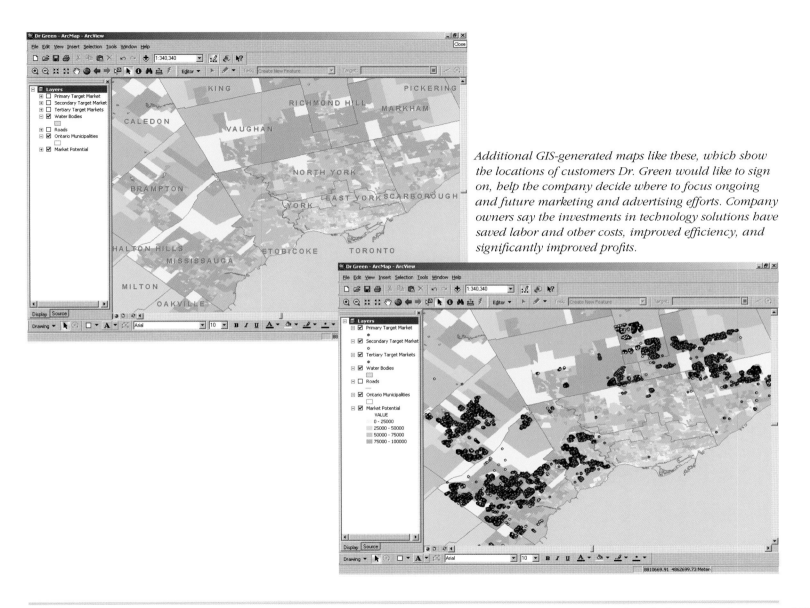

Additional GIS-generated maps like these, which show the locations of customers Dr. Green would like to sign on, help the company decide where to focus ongoing and future marketing and advertising efforts. Company owners say the investments in technology solutions have saved labor and other costs, improved efficiency, and significantly improved profits.

The software

ESRI ArcLogistics Route, and ArcView 8.1 with ArcMap.

The data

CanMap RouteLogistics data, CanMap Streetfile, and demographic census data for Canada.

Acknowledgments

Thanks to Lou Van Haastrecht of Dr. Green Lawncare, Chris Thomas of DMTI Spatial, Inc., and Karl Terrey of ESRI.

The pest extermination industry, like many others, is keenly focused on "zeroing in." No matter what the bug or pest, it needs to be hunted and found, then either killed or otherwise contained, repelled, or removed. Customers, obviously, are far different. Though they need to be hunted and found, they also need to be examined, nurtured, and cloned into new customers. Part of that effort means keeping customers happy with good service at a fair price, and that's why companies periodically analyze their service methods to figure out ways to streamline the work and reduce expenses.

For one industry leader, GIS is playing an ever more important role in the firm's push to understand its various markets. With that knowledge, managers are able to make changes that help cut transportation and other costs, and in turn maintain profitable customer rolls.

The saga of the "Little Man"

Western Exterminator Company was started in 1921 by a young man with just a desk, telephone, and $25 worth of chemicals. Many people recognize the company by its well-known "Little Man" logo mascot—a commanding fellow in top hat, tie, and suit, his large mallet behind him, raising a warning finger to a rodent.

Over the years, Western Exterminator has grown into the largest family-owned-and-operated termite and pest control company in the western United States. It has nearly a thousand employees, including four degreed entomologists and four registered environmental health specialists. With headquarters in Irvine, California, the company provides residential pest control services in California, Arizona, and Nevada, and commercial services nationwide in partnership with others. Structures serviced include homes, apartments, hospitals, nursing homes, schools, retail stores, restaurants, bars, fast food outlets, supermarkets, warehouses, and other commercial and industrial facilities. In recent years, GIS has helped the company improve routing, market analyses, selling of services, and office site location.

Artist Vaughn Kaufman first designed and drew Western Exterminator's logo in 1931. "Kernel Kleenup" was the character's official moniker, but the tag never stuck. Company employees liked calling him the "Little Man," and that's the name that's stayed through the years.

Wide service region

Western Exterminator wrestles with a number of pesky insects and other pests. In addition to the typical assortment of ants, spiders, cockroaches, and flies, there also are rats, mice, and gophers, just to name a few. The mischief and grief they create translates to about 115,000 regular customers for Western Exterminator. To help those customers, the company has about four hundred service vehicles and technicians, each with an average of about three hundred customers per route and territory.

Retail Profit Management (RPM), a consulting firm based in Northridge, California, helped Western Exterminator adopt and use GIS technology. RPM's Web site, www.rpmconsulting.com, provides many examples of its business networking, consulting, and GIS expertise.

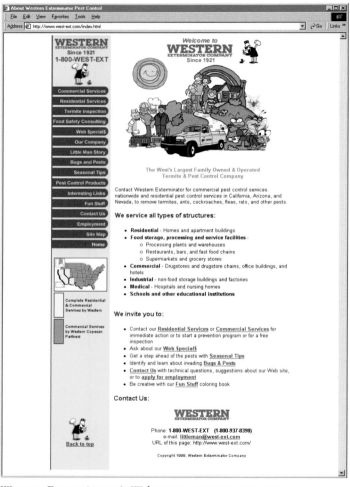

Western Exterminator's Web pages at www.west-ext.com provide a wide variety of information about various pests, along with the services the company provides to combat them.

GIS helps manage

In recent years, Western Exterminator has used GIS software to map and manage its service areas, as illustrated by the maps on this page. Blue areas on a map (top) generated with ESRI's ArcView 3.2 software indicate customers and concentrated market areas, with red markers indicating office locations. The other map (below), also generated with ArcView 3.2, shows the same three-state region, and is the starting point for launching an analysis of any specific market the company wants to study. The GIS allows data and information from tables, such as the one displayed, to be geocoded on the maps. In this example, the map and table are the starting points for examining and changing routing in Phoenix, Arizona.

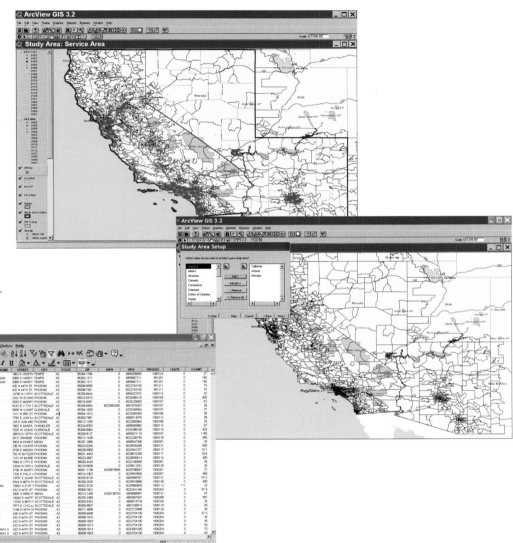

GIS reduces costs

Western Exterminator's two biggest costs are labor and vehicle expenses. Keeping driving time to a minimum increases employee productivity and reduces vehicle wear-and-tear and fuel costs. When technicians are not driving, they have more time for customer problems that require extra attention. Keeping each of its service techs tightly routed within given territories is a high priority; when technicians cross over to other territories, inefficiency creeps in, which is a sign that the company needs to reassign customers or create a new territory serviced by a new technician.

Not long ago, Western Exterminator determined that service routes and territories were beginning to overlap in and around its Phoenix service center. This caused a slip in productivity and increased vehicle costs. GIS was used to analyze routes and reconfigure them, resulting in higher productivity and lower transportation costs.

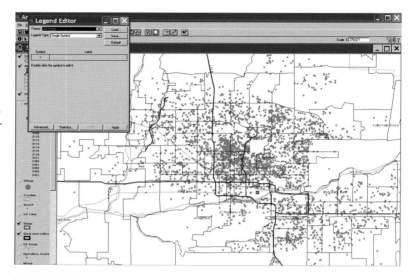

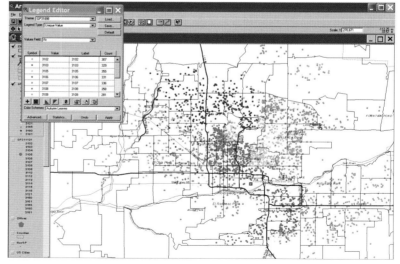

The top map is an initial step that uses green dots to indicate all customers in the Phoenix area. The bottom map is easily produced with a few mouse clicks and uses different colored dots to show stops on different routes.

Closer view of a route

Here's an example of how one service area was reduced in size and made more manageable and profitable. The top map shows the service area before it was reorganized. The area is yellow and covers about thirty-one ZIP Codes; customers are indicated by red dots. After using GIS to reorganize the route and service area, the number of ZIP Codes has been reduced to twenty-five (customers are now represented with blue dots), and the technician has a smaller, more efficiently arranged service area to work.

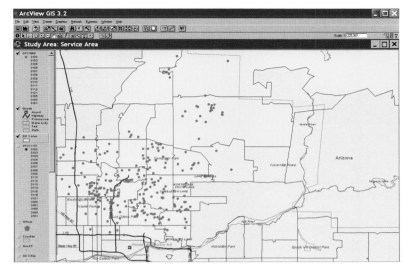

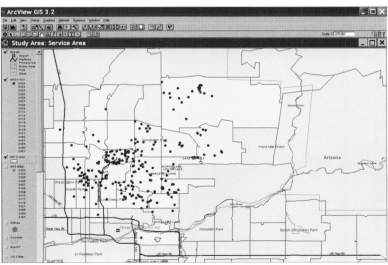

Another route changed

Here, another example of improved route management is illustrated with GIS-generated mapping technology. At the top, the service area and customers are represented in yellow and blue, respectively, and the territory covers twelve large ZIP Code regions. After reorganization, the territory has been reduced to just four ZIP Code areas, except for a small number of customers west of a major highway and just outside the yellow service area. Western Exterminator's managers say the ability to visualize these kinds of changes and manipulate data and maps instantaneously are vital to smart decision making. The color change of the dots helps illustrate the changes and improvements.

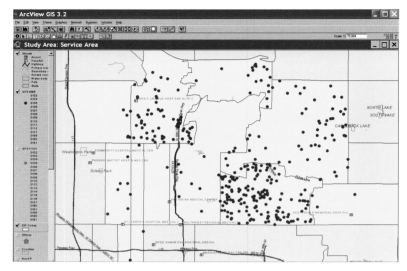

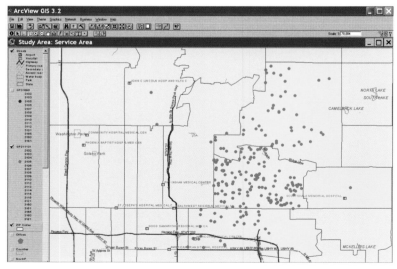

Checking revenues

Western Exterminator uses Business Analyst to balance territories according to how much revenue is produced. Part of the reorganizing includes selecting groups of customers and merging information between tables and maps to obtain quick and easy-to-print total monthly revenue reports that help all members of the management team see what's happening in a given region.

Company officials say GIS software's ability to sort, query, and link information has given Western Exterminator a new way of looking at data and is helping to spur the firm's future growth.

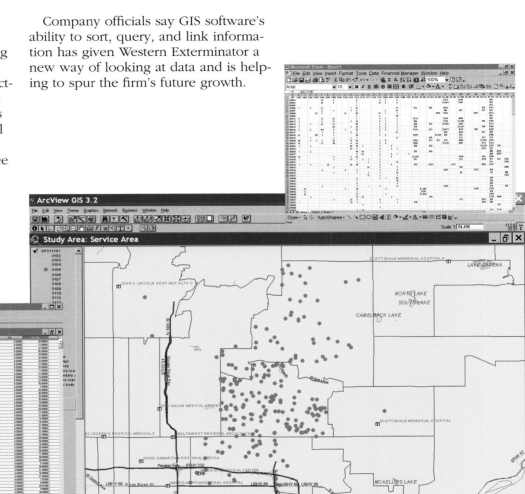

Marketing termite inspections

Western Exterminator also uses GIS-generated maps to help the company win business in the area of termite inspections related to home sales.

Lending institutions commonly require a home to undergo an inspection for termites and wood damage before allowing a loan to go through. Because of that, Western Exterminator works hard to court the real estate industry and obtain the inspection referrals.

Using home sales data pegged to ZIP Codes, Western Exterminator can tell where home sales rates are hottest. The company then determines how much of the inspection and related treatment and repair business it did in specific ZIP Codes. If Western Exterminator's business in those areas isn't at the level the company wants it to be, managers know they have to work harder to develop relationships with real estate brokers and agents who are moving the most properties. In short, managers look for ZIP Codes where they aren't doing many inspections but the maps show a lot of sales activity.

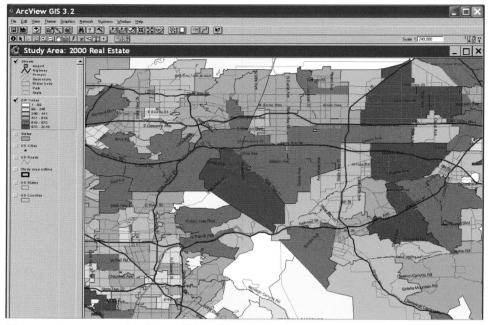

This map is an example of how GIS and business data combine to produce maps that help Western Exterminator market termite inspections and the work that goes along with those inspections. Dark areas are "hot" ZIP Codes where home sales rates are greatest, and that's where Western Exterminator wants to press the real estate industry for the biggest possible share of the inspection business.

The software

Atlas GIS 4.0, ArcView 3.2, ArcView Business Analyst, Crystal Reports®, Microsoft Access, Microsoft Excel, Microsoft Word, Microsoft PowerPoint®, and Centrus™ Geocoder, Sagent Technologies, Inc.

The data

CACI Marketing Systems Group (acquired by ESRI), Geographic Data Technology, Inc. (GDT), infoUSA, and DataQuick®.

Acknowledgments

Thanks to Michael Lawton of Western Exterminator Company, Elio Spinello and Steve Lackow of RPM Consulting, and Jesse Theodore of ESRI.

Finding work and training using GIS

11

Job seekers have long used traditional means to find work—unemployment offices, classified ads in newspapers, kiosk postings, the Yellow Pages, referrals from friends, and cold-calling with resumes in hand. Today, the Internet is making the search smarter, easier, and more comprehensive. In some cases, state and local governments are helping to lead the way.

In the Golden State, legislation designed to create jobs and fill positions with trained, qualified people is gaining notice on a number of fronts. Businesses, along with schools, training centers, and other organizations, are major beneficiaries, as are the thousands of people who find jobs or the training that leads to productive work and satisfying careers. In Los Angeles County, GIS has recently become part of that process.

Regional partnership

The Los Angeles County Regional Workforce Preparation and Economic Development Collaborative is one of six regional partnerships supported by the state of California. In the collaborative's words, the key idea is "to create a comprehensive workforce development system that will integrate the job seeker, employer and education and training communities." Under the Regional Workforce Preparation and Economic Development Act, which seeks to improve economic development, employment, and training services, along with welfare and school reform, the collaborative started a three-year pilot project in the late 1990s with two primary goals in mind. First was the design and development of a single Internet search engine to help job seekers, employers, educators, and skills trainers easily learn about one another. The second goal was to develop a "skills gap profile" of key occupations

in several industries (they currently include metalworking, food preparation, and the apparel industry) so that training opportunities can be enhanced in areas where jobs need to be filled. A recent Internet mapping function has been added to the Workforce's Internet site, and GIS made it possible.

The Los Angeles County Workforce Web site, at www.laworkforce.org, went online in December 2001 in both English and Spanish.

Portal for job seekers

The Workforce's Web page is the starting point for six major categories of information that benefit both the job seeker and the broad network of employers and employment development specialists who can help. The "Finding a Job" category includes information on one-stop centers, online directories, temp agencies, job fairs, government jobs, and military jobs. "Preparing for a Job Search" includes information on writing résumés, posting them, interviewing tips, and salary comparisons. "Information for Employers" explains how companies and organizations can post jobs and find candidates; it also provides information on business assistance and incentives, as well as the labor market. "Career Preparation" has nearly a dozen subcategories ranging from financial aid and scholarships to adult literacy, two- and four-year college programs, online training resources, and adult education. "Employment Support Services" has information on child care and language and interpreter services. And the Web page's "Geographical Industry Search" is the GIS-related tool that leads to interactive explorations for job training and information about the job market.

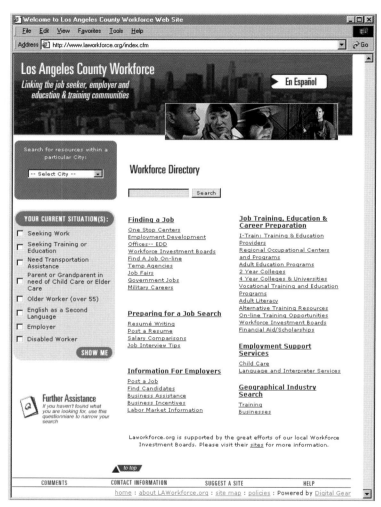

In addition to the six broad categories, the home page lets users check boxes to describe their own situation, such as whether they are seeking work or desiring training. Users can indicate whether they are disabled or otherwise need transportation assistance, or are older workers over the age of 55. Searches also can be narrowed down to particular cities in the region.

Geography as a search agent

The "Geographical Industry Search" is where GIS interactive mapping comes into play on Los Angeles County Workforce's Internet site. A user merely clicks on that heading on the Web page, which brings up the next page indicating either "Training" or "Business." Clicking on "Training" brings up the three current categories available: Metal Manufacturing, Food Preparation, and Apparel Manufacturing.

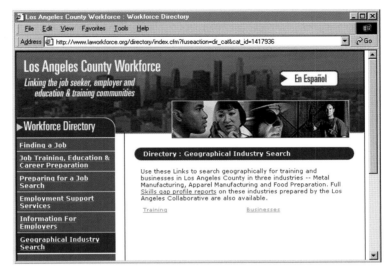

GIS Planning of Berkeley, California, a well-known consulting company in the area of Internet GIS applications for community and economic development, used ESRI's ArcIMS software to develop the geographical industry search component of Los Angeles County Workforce's Web site.

Training in metalworking

Here, a user clicks on "Metal Manufacturing" and is taken to a listing of numerous training opportunities for that field. On a "zoomed out" ArcIMS map, stars indicate a variety of schools and training facilities across Los Angeles County. Clicking on the maps or on the names within the listing provides a "zoomed in" look at more detailed information.

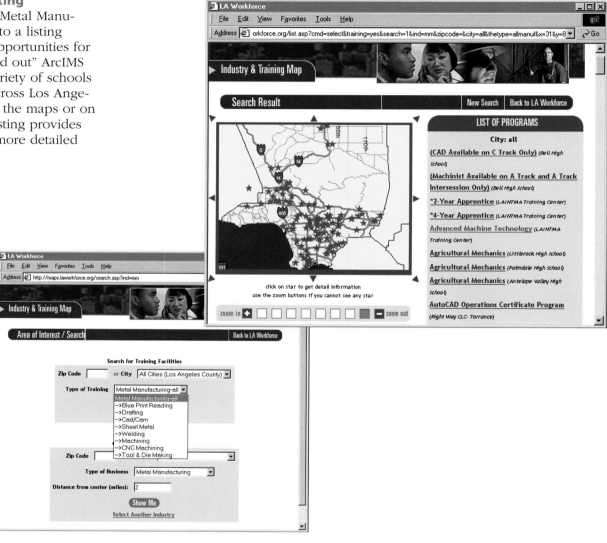

Clicking on the "Advanced Machine Technology" heading in the general listing brings up information on NTMA Training Centers of Southern California, an independent, nonprofit trust that runs schools funded mostly by state money but also by industry donations and students who attend.

As the images on this page illustrate, GIS software helps users see a more detailed locator map, which includes a link to the organization's Web site that provides specific information about the centers, including their courses and programs, as well as tuition and financial aid.

NTMA Training Centers of Southern California (www.trainingcenters.org) has locations in Los Angeles, Orange, and San Bernardino counties. The centers are operated by the Los Angeles chapter of the National Tooling and Machining Association, whose member companies design and manufacture special tools and machines, dies, jigs, fixtures, gauges, and precision-machined parts.

Learning to cook

Food preparation is another of the Workforce's main areas of job training. Starting with the Geographical Industry Search function, a user navigates to interactive maps showing schools and training centers across a wide area of Southern California, along with a lengthy listing. Clicking on a listing of one's interest leads directly to any number of public and private schools, institutions, and training centers.

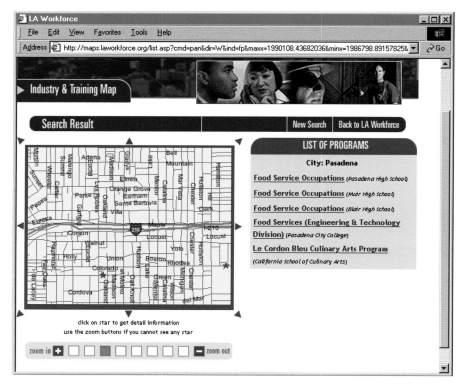

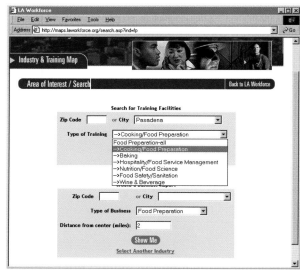

Clicking on "Food Preparation" for all of Los Angeles County generates a long list of schools and training centers, one of which has the mouth-watering heading: "Le Cordon Bleu Culinary Arts Program." Clicking on the name leads to a map showing the location of the California School of Culinary Arts in Pasadena, a leading cooking and baking school. The Los Angeles County Workforce's site links to the school's Web pages, which explain in detail how one trains to become a chef or baker. Many other listings on the Workforce's pages describe programs aimed at general food preparation and kitchen-oriented training.

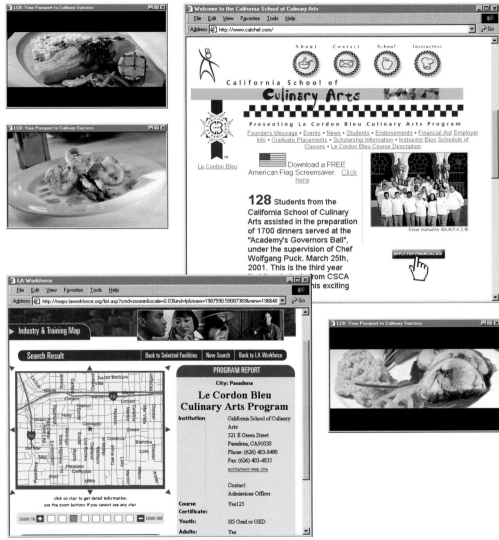

The California School of Culinary Arts (www.calchef.com) offers a program based on the traditions and techniques that evolved during the long history of fine French cuisine.

Hats, coats, and pants

As of early 2002, apparel manufacturing rounded out the three industries for which the Los Angeles County Workforce was offering Web-related services. Clicking on the heading from the Geographical Industry Search page leads to the same types of zoomable maps and copious listings as are offered for metal manufacturing and food preparation. And as with the other categories, the user can click on maps and listing headings to learn more about particular programs of interest.

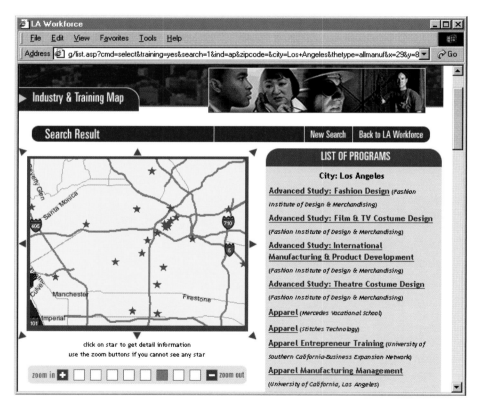

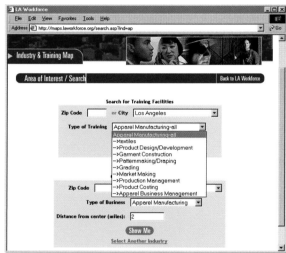

Clicking on "Apparel Manufacturing" for all of Los Angeles County results in a listing that displays "Advanced Study" in four areas: fashion design, film and TV costume design, international manufacturing and product development, and theater costume design. The map for that leads to the Fashion Institute of Design & Merchandising, also known as FIDM, an industry leader. There is also a direct link to FIDM's Web pages.

The Workforce's listing provides names and information on dozens of other schools and programs as well. The search function also lets users hone in on particular aspects of apparel manufacturing; there are job category searches for apparel product design and development, pattern making and draping, production management, and others.

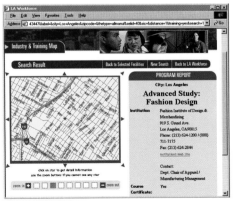

The Fashion Institute of Design & Merchandising, at www.fidm.edu, is a private college that over the past several decades has turned out more than twenty-five thousand graduates in the fields of fashion, graphics, and interior design. Many graduates find work in the entertainment industry worldwide. The school has campuses in Los Angeles, San Francisco, San Diego, and Costa Mesa (Orange County).

Business reports

From the Geographical Industry Search function on the Workforce's Web page, a user can click on "Business" and navigate to a page that launches business reports on the designated industries. These reports, which also contain interactive maps made available by the GIS application in use elsewhere on the site, are intended to show demand for particular types of job trainees. For example, if there is an area of a city in which there is a high density of metal manufacturing businesses—but no training programs—this would show a gap between the available jobs and the available training. This information, in turn, is useful to many of the agencies that make up the Los Angeles County Workforce Collaborative as it plans for future programs.

The collaborative is a partnership of the California Workers Assistance Program AFL-CIO, the state Employment Development Department, Los Angeles Area Chamber of Commerce, Los Angeles County Department of Public Social Services, Los Angeles County Economic Development Corporation, Los Angeles County Office of Education, Los Angeles/Orange County Community Colleges Consortium, and South Bay Workforce Investment Board.

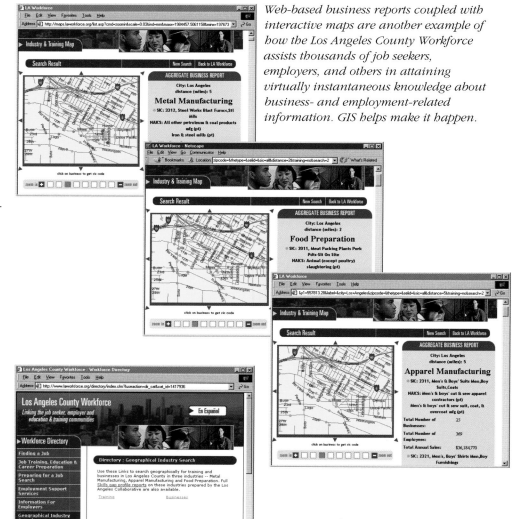

Web-based business reports coupled with interactive maps are another example of how the Los Angeles County Workforce assists thousands of job seekers, employers, and others in attaining virtually instantaneous knowledge about business- and employment-related information. GIS helps make it happen.

The system

The Los Angeles County Workforce's Internet mapping function was developed on a Microsoft Windows 2000 Advanced Server running Internet Information Server 5.0 using ESRI ArcIMS 3.1, Active Server Pages, and Microsoft Access 2000. Development and testing was performed on 866-MHz Dell hardware with 392 MB RAM and a 20-GB hard drive. The site was deployed at the hosting facilities of the California Virtual Campus (CVC) at Rio Hondo Community College on a 900-MHz Dell server with 512 MB RAM and a 20-GB hard drive.

The data

Data for the metal manufacturing, food preparation, and apparel manufacturing training programs is original research, and the data was collected via in-person, telephone, and mail surveys by the Community Development Technologies Center (CD Tech Center) between 1999 and 2001.

Business data was provided by Dun & Bradstreet.

Acknowledgments

Thanks to Linda Wong, Chris Steins, and Carolyn Kingsnorth at the Los Angeles County Regional Workforce Preparation and Economic Development Collaborative, and Anatalio Ubalde and Pablo Monzon at GIS Planning. Thanks also to Steve Albers at LA/NTMA Training Centers of Southern California, Pamela Ramirez at the California School of Culinary Arts, and Shirley Wilson of the Fashion Institute of Design & Merchandising.

12

New opportunities in business education

Businesses that use GIS to solve problems or enhance their operations and profitability need more than computers and software. They also need people who know how to use the technology to its best advantage. In that sense, "GIS and business" involves more than just better marketing, advertising, fleet routing, and site location. It also means better-educated employees and managers. To meet that demand, an increasing number of colleges and universities are offering degrees and certificates in GIS studies, some of them focused specifically on business applications. Software companies, too, are providing an ever-expanding range of educational services devoted to helping business people and others gain greater expertise in GIS.

One school in Nova Scotia, Canada, is an example of this trend in GIS business education, and each year it's turning out graduates who are snapping up jobs on several continents.

Long history in geography

Nova Scotia Community College's Annapolis Valley Campus is about a hundred miles west of Halifax, the capital of Nova Scotia, one of Canada's Maritime Provinces. The Annapolis Valley Campus is comprised of its Middleton site and Lawrencetown site, the latter of which was known originally as the "Survey School," later as the Nova Scotia Land Survey Institute (NSLSI), and still later as the College of Geographic Sciences. Today the Lawrencetown site's Centre of Geographic Sciences (COGS) is the largest trainer of students in the geomatics field in Canada (geomatics being the "acquisition, transformation, management and distribution of geospatially referenced data," according to the school). The Lawrencetown site offers four post-degree geomatics programs in remote sensing, geographic information systems, marine geomatics, and applied geomatics research. In 1997, the school added an advanced diploma in business geographics.

Nova Scotia Community College has fourteen campuses throughout the province; its Web site is at www.nscc.ns.ca. The Annapolis Valley Campus Web address is www.cogs.nscc.ns.ca.

Range of GIS business studies

The Annapolis Valley Campus Web site provides an overview of its business geographics program and the areas of study. Much of the curriculum builds on the initial "Fundamentals of Business Geographics" course, which introduces the basic concepts of GIS as they relate to business. In that class, GIS software is used to present, teach, and solve business-related problems using boundary and street network files, census data, location and marketing databases, and many other kinds of data. Various analytical techniques are taught, including thematic mapping, address matching and geocoding, consumer spotting and profiling, maximizing market potential, and optimizing sales territories.

The wide-ranging curriculum uses a variety of software products, including ArcView and other software developed by ESRI.

Graduates of the COGS program are typically employed in a variety of private businesses and government institutions in such areas as retailing, sales, property management, real estate, health care, tourism, and recreation.

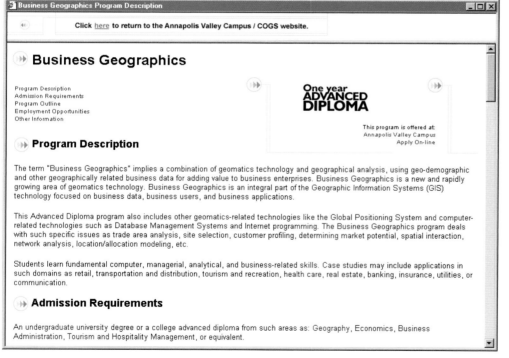

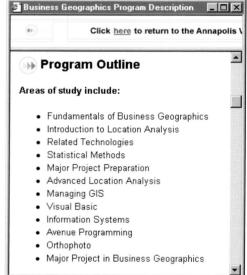

The big challenge

Students embark on many projects during the one-year course of study, but the most important is the "major project." These project concepts are acquired from real companies representing business at local, provincial, national, and international levels. Depending on their complexity, major projects can be completed individually or by a group of students. Skills learned in other courses over the span of two semesters are applied to the major project before the advanced diploma is granted. The school says the major project allows students to handle real-life problems by using data from various sources. Problem-solving skills requiring students to think creatively help prepare them for the job market.

Major projects are presented at the end of the school year during a forum, where local businesses and GIS companies are invited to watch and listen to the students talk about and demonstrate their work.

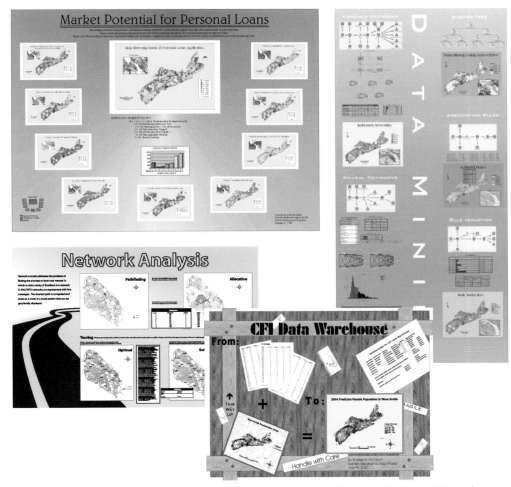

Students' work on major projects are developed into posters that display how GIS and business information are applied to real-world problem solving. Recent major projects have involved such topics as tourism and travel, money loans, data mining and warehousing, and wireless communication markets.

Job prospecting project

One major project by two students focused on defining and evaluating the job market for GIS and business geographics graduates. GIS software was used to study, analyze, graph, chart, and map various kinds of information.

Among the project's conclusions: the highest number of job postings in the United States were in California, Florida, Texas, and Virginia, in that order, and the highest number in Canada were in the provinces of Ontario, British Columbia, Alberta, and Nova Scotia, respectively. The most requested skills for business geographics job postings were mapping and database management, followed by demographic analysis and programming.

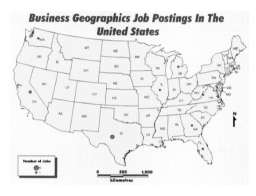

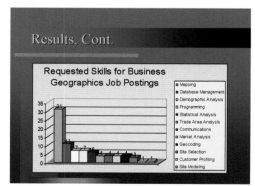

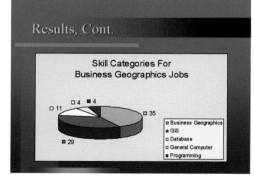

Other programs and resources

The program at Lawrencetown in Nova Scotia is just one that focuses on GIS and business. There are a number of others throughout the world, and the Internet is a good starting point to find them. GeoComm International Corporation, a leading Internet provider of geographic data products, services, and advertising, maintains an extensive listing of GIS-related educational programs on its Web site, ranging from K–12 (for primary- and secondary-level students) to college and university programs, some involving business studies.

One listing is the United Kingdom's University of Leeds, whose School of Geography offers a masters degree in "geographical information systems for business and service planning." The program is an extension of applied research done for many years at the school. Key features of the program include a focus on GIS, geodemographics, retail decision support systems, and working in a business environment outside the school. One module of the program is specifically devoted to learning and using ESRI software.

GeoComm International Corporation's Web site, www.GeoComm.com, provides a listing of educational programs in the United States, Canada, Australia, and elsewhere in the world. The University of Leeds in England has a program devoted to GIS and business, described on its Web site at www.geog.leeds.ac.uk/masters/MABusiness.

On another front, The Center for Advanced Spatial Technologies (CAST), a research group at the University of Arkansas in Fayetteville, provides links to a wide variety of GIS-related educational resources on its Web site, including a link to the "GIS for Business Resource Guide," an extensive listing focusing on GIS and business that's helpful to working professionals as well as students. The "Guide" has topic-specific information on dozens of business-related categories, including advertising research, buying behavior, consumer spending, customer profiling, ethnic markets, retailing, sales and marketing, and trade area analysis, just to name a few.

CAST also has a "Starting the Hunt" site guide to mostly online and free geospatial and attribute data, with links to business and nonprofit organizations.

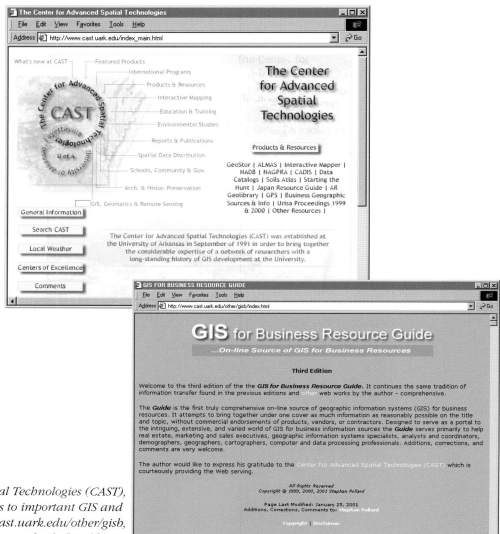

The Center for Advanced Spatial Technologies (CAST), at www.cast.uark.edu, links to important GIS and business guides at www.cast.uark.edu/other/gisb, and www.cast.uark.edu/local/hunt.

Continuing education

ESRI's Virtual Campus (campus.esri.com) offers a six-module course called "Introduction to Successful Marketing using ArcView 3.x." The course, which is aimed at both marketing students and working professionals, demonstrates how public- and private-sector managers can use GIS to analyze markets and use digital geographic data sets to improve decision making. It's another example of how corporations, along with colleges, universities, and other organizations, are using GIS to teach important and highly marketable technological skills to those just entering or already entrenched in the world of business.

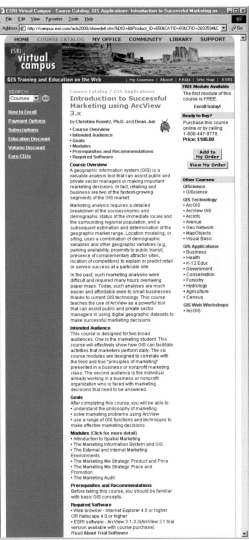

Acknowledgments

Thanks to David Woolnough at Nova Scotia Community College's Annapolis Valley Campus; Glenn Letham at Geo-Comm International Corporation; Steve Carver and Val Marrison at the University of Leeds; Fred Limp at The Center for Advanced Spatial Technology (CAST); Stephan Pollard, developer of the "GIS for Business Resource Guide"; and Brad McCallum of ESRI.

Nova Scotia Community College

Business geographics resources

In many cases, the Internet means never having to leave the home or office to make a trip to the library. Web-based, business-related resources are typically up and running twenty-four hours a day, seven days a week. And, a good supply of Web pages and links can provide hours of informative reading on a wide-ranging array of business topics.

Data is the key

Data is at the heart of every GIS project, and there are a variety of sources in many formats. On the Web, ESRI's data pages, reached via www.esri.com by clicking on the word "data," are one such avenue. There are guidelines for businesses and others regarding selecting and using data, as well as information about data-publishing programs, links to ordering data, and a host of data sources and maps for Internet

users to explore and experiment with. There are links to online resources where users can browse, map, and download free and low-cost data; a partner directory providing a variety of data ready for use with ESRI software; plus additional links to ESRI data and mapping resources, including software products bundled with specific

data sets (these include popular business-related products such as ArcView Business Analyst, ArcLogistics Route, *Business*MAP® PRO, *Route*MAP IMS, and various StreetMap products).

ESRI's Web site links to www.gis.com, a portal to GIS information on the Web. From the GIS.com page, a user can click on "Data for Your GIS" and see topic headings with information that explains data types and models, the importance of data, and how to find, select, and use data to the best advantage.

Geography Network

Another major source of data available through ESRI is the Geography Network (www.geographynetwork.com). Developed and sponsored by ESRI, it's a global network of geographic information users and providers, which facilitates the sharing of data, maps, and information. The Internet is used to deliver interactive maps and downloadable data to users' browsers and desktops. The site is periodically updated with new maps and data features, and users are encouraged to check for the latest additions.

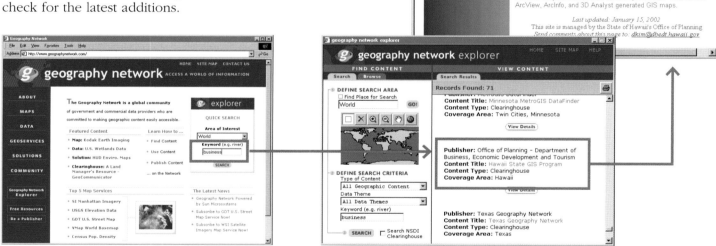

Using the Geography Network's keyword search function and typing in "business," the user is led to dozens of sites and resources, including various clearinghouses that either provide business-related information or demonstrate how GIS is used to help various kinds of businesses. In this example, a user clicks on a listing for the Hawaii Statewide GIS Program from among the listings of business-related offerings. Up pops a Web page for the Hawaii program, with instant connections to maps, data, reports, listings, and other information about Hawaii's business culture, geography, demographics, tourist features, and more.

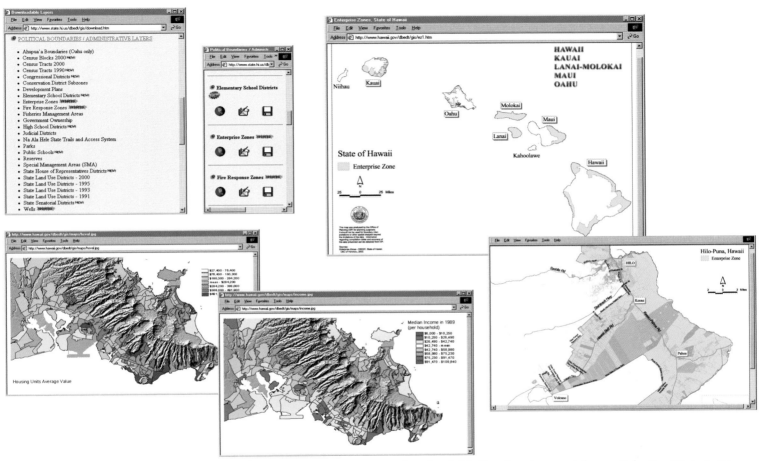

From the Hawaii Statewide GIS Program Web page, a user can access a downloadable list of various map layers. Selecting "Enterprise Zones" leads to a map of the islands' highlighted enterprise zones, which can be enlarged with a zoom feature. Here, the enterprise zone near the city of Hilo, on the island of Hawaii, is shown (far right, lower). Enterprise zones are areas where tax and other incentives are used to stimulate business activity and the creation and preservation of jobs. Many other maps, including those showing income and home values in the city of Honolulu, on the island of Oahu, are available (two maps, lower left). The Hawaii GIS program's Web site also features an interactive mapping function made possible by ArcIMS *software from ESRI.*

Geography Network's Data Downloader function lets users on the Web download free and commercial data, and in some cases make purchases online. In this example, the Data Downloader is used to access an Internet-optimized version of GDT's Dynamap/2000, a database containing more than fourteen million addressed street segments along with postal boundaries, landmarks, and water features. Geography Network users can download up to a dozen ZIP Codes at a time using this street network database, a handy advantage for businesses desiring this type of data and mapping information. The six images here demonstrate how a user, starting with the U.S. map, zeroes in on Las Vegas and some specific ZIP Code areas for which information is desired.

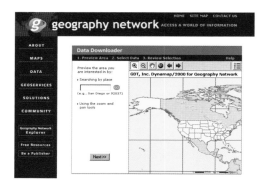

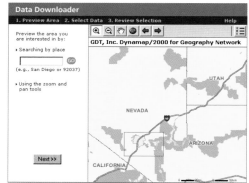

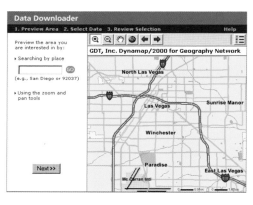

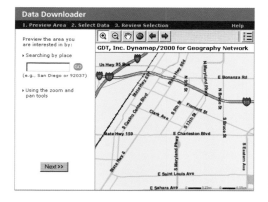

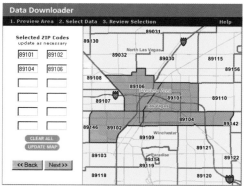

Newest source for data

ESRI Business Information Solutions (also known as ESRI BIS) was formed in early 2002 after ESRI's acquisition of the CACI Marketing Systems Group from CACI International Inc. For businesses and others interested in obtaining business-related data, the ESRI BIS Online Web pages beginning at www.esribis.com provide information on a number of products and services.

From single site-selection reports and segmentation data to more complex marketing analysis systems, the products address a variety of marketing issues, including customer profiling, geocoding, segmenting, site selection, and targeting. There are various databases, reports, and demographics resources, and much of the information is available in electronic formats including diskette and CD–ROM, making it possible to import data into spreadsheets or mapping packages for sorting, ranking, and other manipulations.

ACORN® (A Classification Of Residential Neighborhoods), an important lifestyle segmentation system, is just one example of the products available from ESRI BIS. Users can access ACORN information in a number of ways.

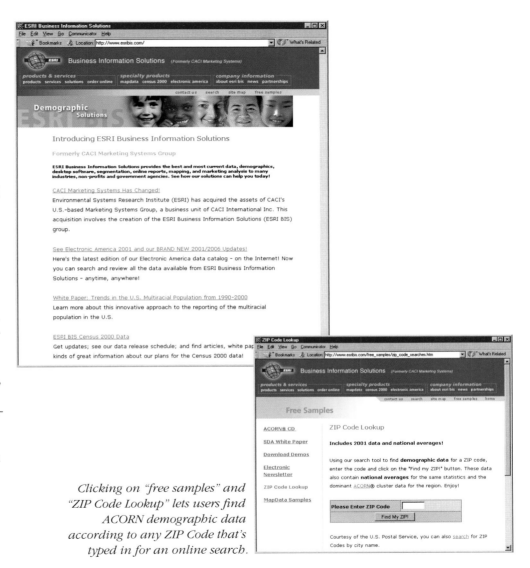

Clicking on "free samples" and "ZIP Code Lookup" lets users find ACORN demographic data according to any ZIP Code that's typed in for an online search.

ACORN's neighborhood segments are divided into forty-three clusters and nine summary groups. This lifestyle classification system is used for market research and site selection by thousands of businesses and organizations in the retail and commercial fields. Many businesses use ACORN data to better understand their customers and markets—then determine where more of those kinds of customers and markets can be found.

In these examples, a ZIP Code search for a part of Seattle, Washington, reveals demographic data for an ACORN group called "Twentysomethings." This group, comprised largely of mobile people in their twenties, completing college or starting careers, is dominant in particular areas of Seattle, as well as many other locales. Information about this group's racial makeup, sex, income, and housing is important to businesses and marketers who might want to target an area with promotional or advertising campaigns. "Twentysomethings" are part of a larger group called "Young Mobile Adults," according to the ACORN system.

Another search, this time for a ZIP Code in Youngstown, Ohio, shows data for an ACORN group known as "Rustbelt Neighborhoods." This category, part of the larger group known as "Factory & Farm Communities," is stable but aging, with concentrations of senior householders. It's a far different group than "Twentysomethings," and businesses like to know where both groups live and work. Data incorporated into GIS mapping systems is a key to selling products and services to these and other ACORN lifestyle and demographic groups.

Post Office: Seattle

Dominant ACORN: 5A (Twentysomethings)

Still unsettled, this market is just completing college or starting their first, postgraduate job. Most are single, mobile, and city dwellers, who are young, active, and urban. Education is the key to this small market's success. Rent is generally below average. This is the second-ranked market for fast food and they are also dieters. They read books, but the media of choice is television.

General Statistics for 2000	ZIP 98104	National
Total Population	10,745	275,247,480
Number of Households	5,203	103,400,199

2000 Population by Race		
White	45.5%	77.9%
Black	25.2%	12.4%
Asian Pacific Islander	23.1%	3.9%
Other	6.2%	5.8%

2000 Population by Gender		
Male	64.7%	48.9%
Female	35.3%	51.1%

2000 Income Figures		
Median Household Income	$18,742	$41,914
HH Income Under $50K	83.5%	59.2%
HH Income $50K-$100K	11.3%	29.8%
HH Income Over $100K	5.2%	11.0%

2000 Housing Figures		
Average Home Value	$432,955	$138,252
Average Rent	$296	$414

Post Office: Youngstown

Dominant ACORN: 7F (Rustbelt Neighborhoods)

This older population resides in the older, industrialized cities and towns of the Northeast and Midwest. They spend money on their homes and their home teams and participate in civic activities. They tend to drive used cars, splurge on lottery tickets, and are top-ranked for using coupons for beauty and household cleaning products. They rank among the highest for watching videos.

General Statistics for 2000	ZIP 44515	National
Total Population	27,271	275,247,480
Number of Households	11,113	103,400,199

2000 Population by Race		
White	93.8%	77.9%
Black	4.8%	12.4%
Asian Pacific Islander	.6%	3.9%
Other	.7%	5.8%

2000 Population by Gender		
Male	47.7%	48.9%
Female	52.3%	51.1%

2000 Income Figures		
Median Household Income	$34,599	$41,914
HH Income Under $50K	72.2%	59.2%
HH Income $50K-$100K	24.8%	29.8%
HH Income Over $100K	3.1%	11.0%

2000 Housing Figures		
Average Home Value	$63,510	$138,252
Average Rent	$311	$414

ACORN CD

ESRI Business Information Solutions offers a free ACORN CD that explains and illustrates how the data is used. It's available by filling out an online form on the ESRI BIS Web site.

Once the CD is received and installed, an Overview function provides a chart showing an example of ACORN segment summaries. There's also an explanation of how the classification system was developed and how it works. A Profiles function gives examples of how the forty-three segments are organized. There are nine summary groups; clicking on different segments reveals how each group is defined and what kinds of people comprise each group. There are charts relating to race, ethnicity, and age; household type, income, and net worth; and education level, occupation, and home value.

The CD also features a navigable list of Purchase Potential Indexes (PPIs), a measure of potential demand for a product or service in a given geographical area. An Applications function examines such questions as how ACORN can help specific businesses and how the system is put to work.

In this example, clicking on ACORN Profiles leads to a page showing the nine demographic summary groups. Placing the mouse over each reveals individual neighborhood types or market segments. In this case, "Upscale Households" contains five clusters. Clicking on "Baby Boomers with Children" lets the user navigate to additional pages that profile this

specific consumer group with text and various bar charts. The Purchase Potential Indexes (PPIs) page shows the various product and service categories for which information and data are available. In this example, clicking on "Appliances" leads to a chart listing various products. If "Bought Charcoal Grill" is highlighted with the mouse, the score of 104 for the "2B"

group ("Baby Boomers with Children") means that this demographic group is 4 percent more likely to purchase this product than average. (Average demand for a product or service is 100 on the PPI. Any score higher than 100 signifies higher-than-average demand by a percentage; scores lower than 100 indicate lower-than-average demand.)

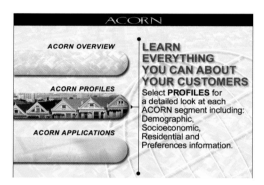

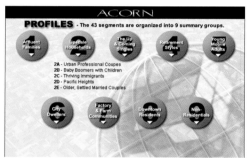

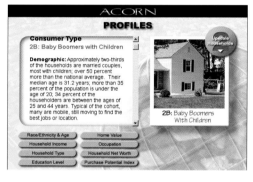

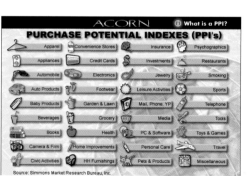

Online resources

The ESRI BIS online store page, which users can link to via www.esribis.com, offers demographic sourcebooks, online reports, and MapData™ products—all important resources for businesses. The sourcebooks, for example, provide detailed information about U.S. ZIP Codes and counties. They are included in many corporate, college, and public libraries, and are used extensively by many business and government agencies. MapData products help users do geocoding, routing, demographic analyses, and thematic mapping.

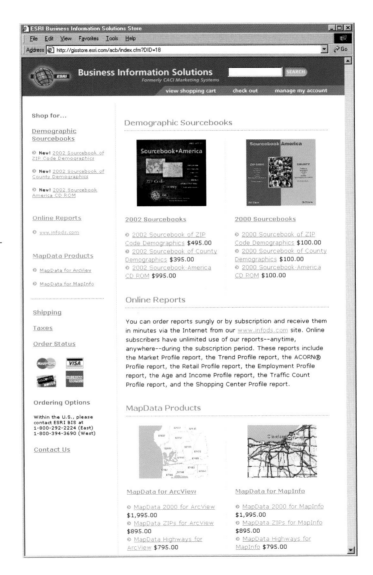

Business specialties

From ESRI's Web page, users can click on "GIS for your specialty" and find information on GIS and its applications in a host of industries and endeavors, including banking and insurance, real estate, and retail and commercial business.

The "Banking and Insurance" page links to topics that figure importantly to the industry, including demographic and competitive analyses, branch location, auditing and compliance issues, and Internet and intranet considerations.

The "Real Estate" specialty page links to information explaining how GIS is helping multiple-listing services, real estate investment trusts, title companies, property appraisers, and the executives, managers, and agents involved in the particulars of both the commercial and residential real estate fields.

The "Retail and Commercial Business" specialty page links to resources dealing with some of the primary GIS-related issues affecting this sphere of the business world, including demographic analyses, customer service, delivery routing, site selection, and marketing.

The specialty pages feature a number of specific business-related GIS software products and how they work in particular ways for the different types of businesses.

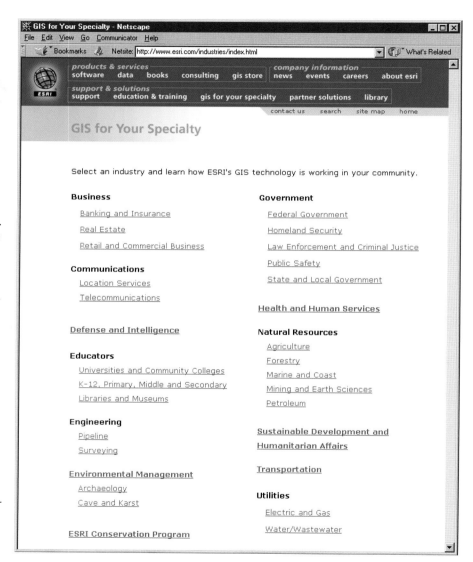

Software

ESRI's "Software" page links to many product pages with explanations, examples, and demonstrations of how particular GIS products can be applied to various kinds of business issues. The "GIS store" page displays what's for sale. A search for "business" produces an even larger page of software, hardware, data, and books that relate to the topic and offer business solutions.

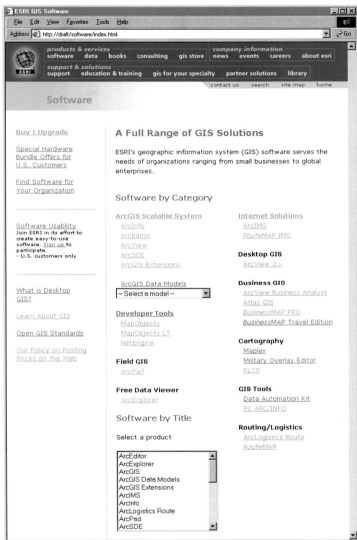

Online libraries

The ESRI Library and Virtual Campus Library pages, along with the "education and training" pages accessible from the ESRI Web site, have multiple resources relating to GIS and business. In addition to search functions, there are listings for white papers, conference proceedings, map collections, brochures, flyers, video clips, demos, journals, magazines, industry-specific references, Virtual Campus courses, live training seminars, Web workshops, and other information.

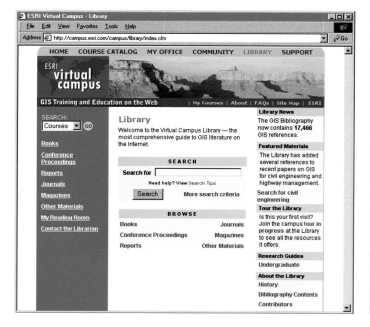

GIS and business bibliography

There are a number of resources, online and in print, offering additional information about GIS and business; some are highlighted here:

The GIS Portal
www.gisportal.com

GIS Development
www.gisdevelopment.net

GEOPlace.com (GEOWorld)
www.geoplace.com

CompInfo, The Computer Information Center
www.compinfo-center.com

Business Geographics, Resources for Economic Geographers
faculty.washington.edu/~krumme/498/Bus.GIS.html

GISCafe.com
www.giscafe.com

GIS for Business Resource Guide
www.cast.uark.edu/other/gisb

GeoCommunity
www.geocomm.com

Bernhardsen, Tor. *Geographic Information Systems: An Introduction*. 2d ed. New York: John Wiley & Sons, Inc., 1999.

Castle, Gilbert H., ed. *GIS in Real Estate: Integrating, Analyzing, and Presenting Locational Information*. Chicago: The Appraisal Institute, 1998.

Davis, Bruce E. *GIS: A Visual Approach*. 2d ed. Albany, N.Y.: OnWord Press, 2001.

Grimshaw, David J. *Bringing Geographical Information Systems Into Business*. 2d ed. New York: John Wiley & Sons, Inc., 1994.

Heywood, Ian, Sarah Cornelius, and Steve Carver. *An Introduction to Geographical Information Systems*. Upper Saddle River, N.J.: Prentice Hall, Inc., 1998.

Longley, Paul, and Graham Clarke, eds. *GIS for Business and Service Planning*. Cambridge: Pearson Professional, Ltd.; New York: John Wiley & Sons, Inc., 1995.

Martin, David. *Geographical Information Systems: Socioeconomic Applications*. 2d ed. London and New York: Routledge, 1996.

Obermeyer, Nancy J., and Jeffrey K. Pinto. *Managing Geographical Information Systems*. New York: The Guilford Press, 1994.

Reeve, Derek, and James Petch. *GIS Organisations and People: A Sociotechnical Approach*. London and Philadelphia: Taylor & Francis, 1999.

Salvaneschi, Luigi. *Location, Location, Location: How to Select the Best Site for Your Business*. Edited by Camille Akin. Central Point, Oreg.: PSI Research/The Oasis Press, 2001.

GIScience

GIS for Everyone SECOND EDITION
Now everyone can create smart maps for school, work, home, or community action using a personal computer. This revised second edition includes the ArcExplorer™ geographic data viewer and more than 500 megabytes of geographic data. ISBN 1-879102-91-9 196 pages

The ESRI Guide to GIS Analysis, Volume 1: Geographic Patterns and Relationships
An important new book about how to do real analysis with a geographic information system. *The ESRI Guide to GIS Analysis* focuses on six of the most common geographic analysis tasks. ISBN 1-879102-06-4 188 pages

Modeling Our World: The ESRI Guide to Geodatabase Design
With this comprehensive guide and reference to GIS data modeling and to the new geodatabase model introduced with ArcInfo™ 8, you'll learn how to make the right decisions about modeling data, from database design and data capture to spatial analysis and visual presentation. ISBN 1-879102-62-5 216 pages

Hydrologic and Hydraulic Modeling Support with Geographic Information Systems
This book presents the invited papers in water resources at the 1999 ESRI International User Conference. Covering practical issues related to hydrologic and hydraulic water quantity modeling support using GIS, the concepts and techniques apply to any hydrologic and hydraulic model requiring spatial data or spatial visualization.
ISBN 1-879102-80-3 232 pages

Beyond Maps: GIS and Decision Making in Local Government
Beyond Maps shows how local governments are making geographic information systems true management tools. Packed with real-life examples, it explores innovative ways to use GIS to improve local government operations. ISBN 1-879102-79-X 240 pages

The ESRI Press Dictionary of GIS Terminology
This long-needed and authoritative reference brings together the language and nomenclature of the many GIS-related disciplines and applications. Designed for students, professionals, researchers, and technicians, the dictionary provides succinct and accurate definitions of more than a thousand terms. ISBN 1-879102-78-1 128 pages

Planning Support Systems: Integrating Geographic Information Systems, Models, and Visualization Tools
Richard Brail of Rutgers University's Edward J. Bloustein School of Planning and Public Policy, and Richard Klosterman of the University of Akron, have assembled papers from colleagues around the globe who are working to expand the applicability and understanding of the top issues in computer-aided planning. ISBN 1-58948-011-2 468 pages

Geographic Information Systems and Science
This comprehensive guide to GIS, geographic information science (GIScience), and GIS management illuminates some shared concerns of business, government, and science. It looks at how issues of management, ethics, risk, and technology intersect, and at how GIS provides a gateway to problem solving, and links to special learning modules at ESRI® Virtual Campus (campus.esri.com). ISBN 0-471-89275-0 472 pages

Mapping Census 2000: The Geography of U.S. Diversity
Cartographers Cynthia A. Brewer and Trudy A. Suchan have taken Census 2000 data and assembled an atlas of maps that illustrates the new American diversity in rich and vivid detail. The result is an atlas of America and of Americans that is notable both for its comprehensiveness and for its precision. ISBN 1-58948-014-7 120 pages

Undersea with GIS
Explore how GIS is illuminating the mysteries hidden in the earth's oceans. Leading-edge applications include managing protected underwater sanctuaries, tracking whale migration, and recent advances in the development of 3-D electronic navigational charts. Companion CD–ROM brings the underwater world to life for both the undersea practitioner and student and includes 3-D underwater flythroughs, ArcView® extensions for marine applications, a K–12 lesson plan, and more. ISBN 1-58948-016-3 276 pages

My Community, Our Earth: A Student Project Guide to Sustainable Development and Geography
Get students involved in an international project about important ideas and practical applications for sustainable development. This book provides guidelines and resources to create a project that could be selected to be on display at the World Summit on Sustainable Development in South Africa in September 2002. For high-school and college students. ISBN 1-58948-039-2 132 pages

CONTINUED ON NEXT PAGE

Other books from **ESRI Press** *continued*

GIScience *continued*

Past Time, Past Place: GIS for History
In this pioneering book that encompasses the Greek and Roman eras, the Salem witch trials, the Dust Bowl of the 1930s, and more, leading scholars explain how GIS technology can illuminate the study of history. Richly illustrated, *Past Time, Past Place* is a vivid supplement to many courses in cultural studies and will fascinate armchair historians. ISBN 1-58948-032-5 224 pages

Mapping Our World: GIS Lessons for Educators
A comprehensive educational resource that gives any teacher all the tools needed to begin teaching GIS technology in the middle- or high-school classroom. Includes nineteen complete GIS lesson plans, a one-year license of ArcView 3.x, geographic data, a teacher resource CD, and a companion Web site. ISBN 1-58948-022-8 564 pages

ESRI Map Book, Volume 16: Geography—Creating Communities
A full-color collection of some of the finest maps produced using GIS software. Published annually since 1984, this unique book celebrates the mapping achievements of GIS professionals. *Directions Magazine* (www.directionsmag.com) has called the *ESRI Map Book* "The best map book in print." ISBN 1-58948-015-5 120 pages

The Case Studies Series

ArcView GIS Means Business
Written for business professionals, this book is a behind-the-scenes look at how some of America's most successful companies have used desktop GIS technology. The book is loaded with full-color illustrations and comes with a trial copy of ArcView software and a GIS tutorial. ISBN 1-879102-51-X 136 pages

Zeroing In: Geographic Information Systems at Work in the Community
In twelve "tales from the digital map age," this book shows how people use GIS in their daily jobs. An accessible and engaging introduction to GIS for anyone who deals with geographic information. ISBN 1-879102-50-1 128 pages

Serving Maps on the Internet
Take an insider's look at how today's forward-thinking organizations distribute map-based information via the Internet. Case studies cover a range of applications for ArcView Internet Map Server technology from ESRI. This book should interest anyone who wants to publish geospatial data on the World Wide Web. ISBN 1-879102-52-8 144 pages

Managing Natural Resources with GIS
Find out how GIS technology helps people design solutions to such pressing challenges as wildfires, urban blight, air and water degradation, species endangerment, disaster mitigation, coastline erosion, and public education. The experiences of public and private organizations provide real-world examples. ISBN 1-879102-53-6 132 pages

Enterprise GIS for Energy Companies
A volume of case studies showing how electric and gas utilities use geographic information systems to manage their facilities more cost effectively, find new market opportunities, and better serve their customers. ISBN 1-879102-48-X 120 pages

Transportation GIS
From monitoring rail systems and airplane noise levels, to making bus routes more efficient and improving roads, this book describes how geographic information systems have emerged as the tool of choice for transportation planners. ISBN 1-879102-47-1 132 pages

GIS for Landscape Architects

From Karen Hanna, noted landscape architect and GIS pioneer, comes *GIS for Landscape Architects*. Through actual examples, you'll learn how landscape architects, land planners, and designers now rely on GIS to create visual frameworks within which spatial data and information are gathered, interpreted, manipulated, and shared. ISBN 1-879102-64-1 120 pages

GIS for Health Organizations

Health management is a rapidly developing field, where even slight shifts in policy affect the health care we receive. In this book, you'll see how physicians, public health officials, insurance providers, hospitals, epidemiologists, researchers, and HMO executives use GIS to focus resources to meet the needs of those in their care. ISBN 1-879102-65-X 112 pages

GIS in Public Policy: Using Geographic Information for More Effective Government

This book shows how policy makers and others on the front lines of public service are putting GIS to work—to carry out the will of voters and legislators, and to inform and influence their decisions. *GIS in Public Policy* shows vividly the very real benefits of this new digital tool for anyone with an interest in, or influence over, the ways our institutions shape our lives. ISBN 1-879102-66-8 120 pages

Integrating GIS and the Global Positioning System

The Global Positioning System is an explosively growing technology. *Integrating GIS and the Global Positioning System* covers the basics of GPS and presents several case studies that illustrate some of the ways the power of GPS is being harnessed to GIS, ensuring, among other benefits, increased accuracy in measurement and completeness of coverage. ISBN 1-879102-81-1 112 pages

GIS in Schools

GIS is transforming classrooms—and learning—in elementary, middle, and high schools across North America. *GIS in Schools* documents what happens when students are exposed to GIS. The book gives teachers practical ideas about how to implement GIS in the classroom, and some theory behind the success stories. ISBN 1-879102-85-4 128 pages

Disaster Response: GIS for Public Safety

GIS is making emergency management faster and more accurate in responding to natural disasters, providing a comprehensive and effective system of preparedness, mitigation, response, and recovery. Case studies include GIS use in siting fire stations, routing emergency response vehicles, controlling wildfires, assisting earthquake victims, improving public disaster preparedness, and much more. ISBN 1-879102-88-9 136 pages

Open Access: GIS in e-Government

A revolution taking place on the Web is transforming the traditional relationship between government and citizens. At the forefront of this e-government revolution are agencies using GIS to serve interactive maps over their Web sites and, in the process, empower citizens. This book presents case studies of a cross-section of these forward-thinking agencies. ISBN 1-879102-87-0 124 pages

GIS in Telecommunications

Global competition is forcing telecommunications companies to stretch their boundaries as never before—requiring efficiency and innovation in every aspect of the enterprise if they are to survive, prosper, and come out on top. The ten case studies in this book detail how telecommunications competitors worldwide are turning to GIS to give them the edge they need. ISBN 1-879102-86-2 120 pages

Conservation Geography: Case Studies in GIS, Computer Mapping, and Activism

This collection of dozens of case studies tells of the ways GIS is revolutionizing the work of nonprofit organizations and conservation groups worldwide as they rush to save the earth's plants, animals, and cultural and natural resources. As these pages show clearly, the power of computers and GIS is transforming the way environmental problems and conservation issues are identified, measured, and ultimately, resolved. ISBN 1-58948-024-4 252 pages

GIS Means Business, Volume Two

For both business professionals and general readers, *GIS Means Business, Volume Two* presents more companies and organizations, including a chamber of commerce, a credit union, colleges, reinsurance and real estate firms, and more, who have used ESRI software to become more successful. See how businesses use GIS to solve problems, make smarter decisions, enhance customer service, and discover new markets and profit opportunities. ISBN 1-58948-033-3 188 pages

CONTINUED ON NEXT PAGE

Other books from **ESRI Press** *continued*

ESRI Software Workbooks

**Understanding GIS: The ARC/INFO® Method
(UNIX®/Windows NT® version)**
A hands-on introduction to geographic information system technology. Designed primarily for beginners, this classic text guides readers through a complete GIS project in ten easy-to-follow lessons. ISBN 1-879102-01-3 608 pages

Understanding GIS: The ARC/INFO Method (PC version)
ISBN 1-879102-00-5 532 pages

ARC Macro Language: Developing ARC/INFO Menus and Macros with AML
ARC Macro Language (AML™) software gives you the power to tailor ARC/INFO Workstation software's geoprocessing operations to specific applications. This workbook teaches AML in the context of accomplishing practical ARC/INFO Workstation tasks, and presents both basic and advanced techniques. ISBN 1-879102-18-8 826 pages

Getting to Know ArcView GIS
A colorful, nontechnical introduction to GIS technology and ArcView software, this workbook comes with a working ArcView demonstration copy. Follow the book's scenario-based exercises or work through them using the CD and learn how to do your own ArcView project. ISBN 1-879102-46-3 660 pages

Extending ArcView GIS
This sequel to the award-winning *Getting to Know ArcView GIS* is written for those who understand basic GIS concepts and are ready to extend the analytical power of the core ArcView software. The book consists of short conceptual overviews followed by detailed exercises framed in the context of real problems. ISBN 1-879102-05-6 540 pages

Getting to Know ArcGIS Desktop: Basics of ArcView, ArcEditor, and ArcInfo
Getting to Know ArcGIS Desktop is a workbook for learning ArcGIS™, the newest GIS technology from ESRI. Readers learn to use the software that forms the building blocks of ArcGIS: ArcMap™ for displaying and querying maps; ArcCatalog™ for managing geographic data; and ArcToolbox™ for setting map projections and converting data. Richly detailed illustrations and step-by-step exercises teach basic GIS tasks. Includes a fully functioning 180-day trial version of ArcView 8 software on CD–ROM, as well as a CD of data for working through the exercises. ISBN 1-879102-89-7 552 pages

ESRI educational products cover topics related to geographic information science, GIS applications, and ESRI technology. You can choose among instructor-led courses, Web-based courses, and self-study workbooks to find education solutions that fit your learning style and pocketbook. Visit www.esri.com/education for more information.

ESRI Press publishes a growing list of GIS-related books. Ask for these books at your local bookstore or order by calling 1-800-447-9778. You can also shop online at www.esri.com/gisstore. Outside the United States, contact your local ESRI distributor.

ESRI Press • 380 New York Street • Redlands, California 92373-8100 • www.esri.com/esripress